ONE NIGHT STAND

by the same author

LIEBESTRAUM
LEAVING LAS VEGAS

ONE NIGHT STAND

Mike Figgis

faber and faber

First published in 1997
by Faber and Faber Limited
3 Queen Square London WC1N 3AU

Photoset by Parker Typesetting Service, Leicester
Printed in England by Clays Ltd, St Ives plc

Faber and Faber would like to thank Amanda Blue
for the assistance she provided in making
this publication possible.

A CIP record for this book
is available from the British Library
ISBN 0-571-19407-9

2 4 6 8 10 9 7 5 3 1

CONTENTS

THE DYNAMICS OF FILM
A Conversation between Mike Figgis and Walter Donohue

I first met Mike Figgis in 1970 when we were both lucky enough to be working in Fringe Theatre – I say 'lucky' because the excitement of being involved in theatre at that time was akin to that which film-makers feel in the nineties. I eventually left the theatre and moved over to Channel Four, where Mike approached me about a proposal he had in mind: turning his performance piece, *The House*, into a film. Although Mike's film experience was limited, it was exactly the kind of innovative project for which Channel Four had come into existence. Channel Four funded the venture, it was a success, it led to *Stormy Monday*, and the rest, as they say, is history.

On the release, and publication of the screenplay, of *Liebestraum* in 1991, Mike and I sat down and talked about his career up to that point. This conversation carries on from there.

WALTER DONOHUE: *How did the script of* One Night Stand *come your way?*

MIKE FIGGIS: After *Basic Instinct* came out, Joe Eszterhas teamed up with Adrian Lyne (director of *Fatal Attraction*) and they created a bidding war on a synopsis – not even a script – called *One Night Stand*. For perfectly understandable reasons, all the studios entered into this bidding war, and something between three and four million dollars were paid by New Line on the basis of a two-page treatment. So they then had this project which Eszterhas had to turn into a script. Somewhere between that point and the point where I came into the picture, Adrian Lyne left the project and New Line was left with a very expensive treatment and no director, and for a studio this was a real disaster. Although the status of the writer has escalated out of all recognition over the past ten years – one might say significantly through Eszterhas's efforts – you still need a director on board to provide the heat. At the same time as they lost the director, Eszterhas's Las Vegas film – *Show Girls* – came out – a film which everyone had eagerly anticipated because they thought it was going to be a very erotic, tough movie like *Basic Instinct*, albeit with two unknown actors. Then, of course, the film received the worst reviews in Hollywood's history and, more catastrophically, was a box-office disaster. So it was the worst time for a company to be backing an expensive Joe Eszterhas script. It was embarrassing.

About this time (before *Leaving Las Vegas* came out) the script was doing the rounds. I read it on holiday, avidly, from cover to cover, in complete astonishment that anyone would think that the film could be made without entering the world of hardcore pornography. That script was basically about having sex, though there were some other scenes where the main character agonizes with his wife, and then goes back again to his lover, and there's more sex. But the way the sex was described was so graphic, and, given the repetition of the sex, one would have had to shoot it with some kind of variety, otherwise you'd be showing the same kind of typical, abstract sexual scene. So I was puzzled how anyone who'd read the script at the studio thought they could ever make it without getting into such censorship problems that would stop them making money on it. So I passed. Not that it was being offered to me in a hard way; there was certainly no heat on my career at this point. Then *Leaving Las Vegas* came out and, suddenly, I was flavour of the day. And at that point New Line re-submitted the script and asked if I would come in for a meeting.

I went to New Line and said that I was not interested in the script at all but that there was something about its structure that I really did like and asked if they were prepared to let me do a 'page one' rewrite. I told them that what I proposed to do was so radical that I didn't know why they would want to do it, since they had already paid millions of dollars for a script. What I was suggesting was throwing it out and retaining only the title and three-act structure. They said they would go along with that. About this time I had been talking to John Calley (head of MGM at the time of *Leaving Las Vegas* and then head of Sony) about doing a remake of Truffaut's penultimate film, *The Woman Next Door*, but then I had second thoughts. It would have been arrogant to assume one could have improved upon it. But, then I thought about the *One Night Stand* structure in simple terms – the rewrite, that is. In Act One a married man who lives in LA goes to New

York and through various circumstances – through fate – has a one night adulterous affair. But in his and his partner's mind it is nothing they would pursue beyond this one night. In Act Two he goes back to LA and we see that he's really not very happy or fulfilled in what he's doing and in Act Three, through a quirk of fate, he's back in New York and is reunited with the woman he's spent the night with. The third act resolves the first and second acts. This is basically the three-act structure of the Eszterhas script and, although it's a very simple idea, funnily enough those three-act structural ideas are quite rare. Possibly because the Truffaut film was on my mind, it gave me the idea that it was possible to genuinely do a rewrite on this that would make the film function better. Of course, when it was announced in *Variety* and the *Hollywood Reporter* that I was going to do a Joe Eszterhas film – that's how it was labelled – I recall meeting people who had read the announcement and were quite shocked. They said things like, 'Well, no doubt you'll be really well paid', and 'We understand'. But you could see that they were disappointed in seeing me go from something as independent as *Leaving Las Vegas* to such a crass (in their minds) financially based decision. So that's the history of the script.

At the end of the last interview we did – for the publication of the screenplay of Liebestraum *– I asked you: 'What are you going to do next?' and you replied, 'I'm not sure, but whatever it is, there'll be some kind of darkness in it.' And from there you went from* Mr Jones, *which is about a manic depressive, then* The Browning Version, *which is concerned with failure, and* Leaving Las Vegas, *which is about a man who drinks himself to death. So do you feel that your decision to do* One Night Stand *was a continuation of that? That you were investigating what happens to people when they get involved in these very elemental situations? You said that the original script was crass, but that there was something underneath that you responded to.*
Ultimately, it's about adultery. And therefore it's about the very heart of male–female, or physical relationships, regardless of gender. It's about adult relationships and how they work and how they don't work. Certainly, in the culture we live in, economics is rarely the dominant reason why people stay together. So, one has the luxury of examining the reasons why people – I mean the

middle classes – are together or ought not to be together. As a basis for any kind of story, that was interesting. There's a film-maker – if it's not Bergman, then it's another European film-maker – who said that he didn't think that his stories were so dark. I agree. I think my stories are just realistic.

The story of *Leaving Las Vegas* was extreme in that it dealt with a kind of suicidal alcoholism, but along the road, the main character was very humane. Others have found in my films a kind of sadness or depression associated with the characters, but I've always thought that that's life. And within the film there's humour and compassion. In a lot of American films the manic attempt to be cheerful seems to me somewhat insane, and certainly disturbing. Also, in the tradition of literature I grew up with, there's nothing unusual about such a realistic depictions of life. It's only in cinema that there's this insane chirpiness.

One of the differences between Liebestraum *and* One Night Stand *is that in* Liebestraum *the main characters – the man and woman – are drawn together as if by fate. There's nothing they can do about it, and this relationship has repercussions on those around them; there's a kind of violence that is unleashed because of this attraction between the two characters. In* One Night Stand, *however, something seems to have happened in the intervening years and the repercussions don't lead to violence but seem to move towards another plane, since what they find in the relationship is something special and rare, which is why they have to be together.*

Maybe there's a more simple explanation in that film-making is extremely difficult and your control of it as a medium is such a subtle thing – it has a lot to do with experience and your own security. So when you first come into films one of the things most young film-makers do is to try to exert control through style. The characters become prisoners of the film and the emotion comes out most strongly through the director rather than through the performances of the actors. It's now ten years since I made my first film and in that time a lot of things have happened to me. Also, in terms of film-making skills, I feel much more secure as a director now, which means I'm more capable of letting go of certain 'auteur' elements. As human beings get older – like jazz musicians – their style becomes more minimal. Their phrasing becomes shorter, more poetic. That's something I've been aware of and have aspired to – a more minimalist, relaxed participation in whatever I'm doing.

Does this letting actors have more freedom account for the fact that in both Leaving Las Vegas *and in* One Night Stand *there are passages of dialogue that are different in the completed film from what was on the page of the screenplay?*
Yeah.

I imagine the scene around the dinner table was approached in that way.
In both that scene and in the marketing scene, I was using, in cameo form, incredibly talented actors, a lot of whom I already knew, like John Ratzenberger, whom everyone knows from *Cheers.* But, in fact, he was very much part of the London alternative scene in the seventies at the same time as *The People Show.* He was in a company called Sal's Meat Market, who were a very radical, very funny, very surreal comedy group that was fifteen years ahead of its time. So, to have him come on board to do this cameo was great because I knew his improvisational skills were incredible. So, if you have the likes of Amanda Donohoe and Thomas Hayden Church, with an ensemble of actors on that kind of improvisational level, you know that they're going to come up with something that is far better than the script. Once we start shooting I hardly open the script. Since I've written it I know the sense of the scene and, even though the actors have learned their lines, because I'm not looking at the script the actors know I'm not anal about script retention. So things flow a lot better with the script serving more as a blueprint.

But do you guide the actors in the sense that you know, generally, the point the scene has to make, so if the actors use different words to get to that, it's okay? Or do you abandon the point of the scene if the actors begin pushing it in a different direction?
It's completely open. The only thing that functions for me is a kind of inbuilt meter that says that the scene's playing way too long and the actors are starting to waffle – something that always happens when they improvise – taking one very sharp line and making it three times longer because they're enjoying the punch-

line. I'll think to myself, it is quite funny, but it's going to be very hard to cut it down in the edit because they're going to lose their flow. So I'll say: 'Look this is going really well but it's actually three times too long, so let's do it again and really cut it down to the bone now that everyone really understands the scene.' I personally don't care by what verbal means the actors get to the point. Sometimes I will say that there was something in the script that was actually funnier, now that I've heard all the choices. And it's a trade-off because they will always get something in that they've created.

Did you use that same approach in the scene following the dinner party: the argument between Max and his wife?
Yeah.

But the requirements for that scene are obviously quite different from those for the dinner party scene; the difference between repartee and raw emotion.
There are two things I wanted to capture in both those scenes. In the dinner party scene I wanted to capture LA socially, and there were very specific ground rules dictated by the kind of characters that were sitting round the table, how they were defined and how they felt about each other. All the actors either live in LA or have spent some time there, so there was something for them to enjoy since we had all been to that dinner party in some shape or form. So I set up a very interesting way of shooting the scene with the cinematographer, Declan Quinn. We built a scaffold pipe rig above the dinner party and hung a kind of soft light from it so that we could film anybody at any given moment. Declan has a system, which I call Bunjee-Cam, where you hang the camera off a bunjee attached to the scaffolding and you can hold a 35mm camera with one hand. We ran two cameras (which we did pretty much all the time). I operated the second camera. Normally, when you do a scene which involves eight speaking actors and you want to create that dinner party atmosphere where everyone is talking at the same time, your conventional choice would be to shoot singles on everyone with nobody else saying anything, then create the overlaps in the edit afterwards. But it's a very artificial device, so I said to the actors: don't worry about overlaps, just go as naturalistically as possible and I'll deal with it in the edit, and,

although I'll give the editor heartache, I know it'll be fine. I thought that if you ran two cameras – and we were sometimes running three with another operator on a longer lens – I could negotiate with Declan how we cover the actors so that we could do action cuts on existing dialogue. It's a very long scene, so we allowed two whole days. But I'd always said to the first assistant that I thought it'd go much quicker. In fact, we shot the whole thing in less than a night and when I saw the dailies I was delighted because it had a documentary feel to it. So, that was the essence of what I wanted to catch from that scene. In the following sequence I wanted to capture the feeling of a marital row, something that's been building up for months and triggered specifically by bad behaviour at the dinner party, as perceived by Max's wife. In fact, in the script there were two or three scenes that took place after the marital row, which dealt with the family, the continuing chasm between the husband and wife and the break-up of their marriage. But when I saw the results of the fight between the two of them, it was so clearly a cutting point to get out of the second act that I decided to let the other scenes go. I'm always aware of the possibility of losing scenes later on, and one *should* be losing scenes since film is a reductive process.

So how did you come to cast Wesley Snipes?
I originally wrote this for Nic Cage, as a logical extension of *Leaving Las Vegas*. We'd both said it would be great to work together again but he was very disturbed by the script. He'd just got married and he didn't want to take on the subject of adultery, since, as an actor, if he took on the part, it was something he'd want to do in a deeply personal and realistic way. It's probably one of the best reasons for not doing a script that I've ever heard. I completely respected Nic's decision, but it slightly floored me in the sense that I suddenly had to go out and look for an actor when, in my mind, there had never been any agenda. I felt I'd found an actor I could work with quite happily on four films in a row. He's such a brilliant actor. Also, Nic was a kind of security for me, since even if it was a 'Joe Eszterhas script', I'd be going in with my team and have the protection of my 'film family'. So there I was, apparently doing a very commercial, sexist script and was on the open market with actors again. And I went from this

paradoxical situation where everybody in town said: 'There isn't an actor in the world who won't want to work with you, because your last two actors both got nominated for Oscars – and one of them won' to a situation where I literally couldn't get an actor because I'd gone down the path of writing it for Nic, I was then looking for Nic Cage substitutes. I was going to the likes of John Malkovitch, John Cusack and Sean Penn, but they were all very wary of the Eszterhas factor. Ironically, the three actors I wanted all ended up making the same movie: *Con Air* (Cage, Cusack and Malkovitch). I was becoming very frustrated and one night said to the producer, Annie Stewart, 'Isn't it ironic that there are all these black actors out there, who don't get enough work, and then when I come from such a fêted film as *Leaving Las Vegas*, I cannot get a young white male actor to set foot into the film.' I heard my own voice saying this and – my own limitations stun me sometimes – I thought: 'Why am I not offering it to black actors?' And in my dialogue with myself I answered: 'Because I wrote it white.' And my other voice said: 'So what? What actually is the difference?' Obviously there are psychological, cultural, racial differences that are inbred in everyone, but I suddenly became very excited by the idea of opening the door and going down that corridor. So that's what I did. The first actor I thought of was Wesley, and Annie and I met him for a cup of coffee. He hadn't read the script and I was as honest as I could be. I said to him: 'I'm not trying to be black. I don't want this to be about black and white. I just want the best actor. And my own racial shortcomings have prevented me from looking at the film in this wider way – which is typical of the way we make films anyway. So I'll be honest with you about that and part of that honesty is that I'm not going to rewrite the script if you say you're going to do it. I'm not going to rewrite it as a black character.' And when he said (some days later) that he would do it, he and I looked at the overall casting in terms of who he could be married to, and so on. Although it didn't change the script, it did, up to a point, change the way of looking at it.

But casting Wesley Snipes did have an effect on how you approached the photography of the film.

Wesely was very practical about the problems of photographing black actors in relation to white actors. He'd been in a number of films where, even if the dominant number of actors on the screen were black, the DP would still expose for the white faces and allow the black faces to become featureless and mask-like. DPs get frightened of black skin. If we take, for example, a scene with Wesley Snipes and Nastassja Kinski.

You mean one of the night-time scenes?
Actually, the night-time scenes are easier, in a way. But if you take something in bright light, you might get maybe three or four stops difference in exposure from Wesley, who has very dark, black skin. And Nastassja is very Northern European, very fair.

But why was it easier in a night-time scene like the one where they're kissing in the hospital room?
Well, at least there you can aesthetically take the light levels down on Nastassja's face and still get an exposure on her and, at the same time, help the lighting on Wesley's skin without appearing to have somehow lit the difference. Whereas in bright sunlight, for example, you don't have a lot of elements to help you. You have one, very dominant, open source – the sun. You don't want to inhibit the performance by having to light one actor individually and so lock yourself in to a series of close-ups, thereby losing the possibility of having the actors in the same frame. You enter into the world of narcissistic lighting that is associated with Hollywood divas. Wesley was very aware of the problem and, given the nature of what he was setting out to do when we did the first lighting tests, there was a very difficult moment when he came into the screening room for the tests Declan Quinn and I had done *in extremis*. We'd said, let's see what happens when we don't use any light. We wanted to see the bad news. It was a mistake on my part to involve Wesley in the screening of those tests. We didn't know each other well enough at that point to trust each other. So what he saw was the cliché of the black man disappearing on screen, but it was good because his reaction was pretty passionate and we realized that we had to come up with a system that is naturalistic (because I didn't want a 'lit' look to the film), but which never gives us this problem. So that's what we did.

Could you talk about how you cast Nastassja Kinski?
I had always really admired Nastassja's work and thought that she was an actress who was unpredictable and yet believable. No one really takes her seriously in America, but as far as I was concerned there was definitely an aura about her, probably harking back to *Paris, Texas.* So I arranged to meet her and we had a very involved conversation about the script, which was more than strange. I'd ask her questions and her answers were very peculiar. There was obviously something wrong. So I asked her to describe the opening scene in the script and when she did I realized that her agent had given her the original Joe Eszterhas draft. And I said to her, 'My God, you read that script and you still turned up for the meeting? I'm really flattered.' And she said, 'Well, I saw your film and I really wanted to meet you and I'd love to work with you.' So I said, 'I think we should stop the meeting now and I'd really like you to read the other script before we talk again.' And that's what we did. She turned up again, highly relieved. I still wonder how she thought she was going to do that other film, but I admire her bravery for coming to the meeting despite the script. She had managed, she said, to extract some heart from it; she understood the character and that it was about love and not just sex.

I was surprised by how little you know about Karen's character. You know all you need to know about Max; not just because he talks to the audience, but because you actually see him in action. You see him dealing with his colleagues at work, with his wife and children, whereas Karen seems mysterious at first, but as the film goes on you don't actually learn very much more about her, except that she's some kind of scientist. Was this blankness conscious on your part?
I hadn't really thought of it like that, but I can answer the question in a practical way. In the first act there isn't any time to find out anything about Karen. Also the nature of their relationship is based on the fact that they know nothing about each other and they agree (it was in the script, but not in the film) not to exchange telephone numbers or anything other than their first names. So that took care of the first act. Karen's not in the second act, which is strongly from Max's point of view. He's under siege from his emotions because his best friend's dying. Then he bumps into his lover again, only to discover she's related by marriage to his best

friend. And then his wife comes in, which completely excludes the possibility of schematic dialogue between them. There's an inhibition about their relationship which carries on until the very end. The one time they have a private dialogue it has to be whispered because they're in a sick man's room. The focus at that point has to be how they feel about each other. The audience has to know that they care for each other. So there's no room in the film and I felt that any time spent giving a back-story about Karen and how she felt would deflate the tension of the emotion. One could say the same thing about Elisabeth Shue in *Leaving Las Vegas*. You really don't know very much about her, other than how she feels about the Nic Cage character.

Back-story has become a device to spoonfeed an audience with information that they think they need. I've always felt that if you cast the right actor, you'll get a kind of emotional taste of what kind of person they are and that's enough.

Elia Kazan once said that acting was about listening. If an actor is a good listener you actually learn a great deal about them by the way they listen, which is what Nastassja Kinski is very good at.

John Gielgud said about great acting that it was the ability to do nothing, with meaning. Nastassja was frustrated by the lack of opportunity within her character to express herself more, but then again she's not the best person to judge her own power on screen. Often an actor suspects it's a back-handed compliment when you say that their presence is so strong that they don't need to do anything. To me, film is like meeting people. Your receptors are stimulated because you're seeing and appreciating someone physically and mentally for the first time and you're finding them attractive – or unattractive – in various ways. But you will never have quite the same sharpness of judgement because by the tenth time you meet them there will be a familiarity there. Someone you found absolutely, rivetingly interesting and attractive will, perhaps, seem quite ordinary by the tenth meeting. The beauty of film is that you can approximate that in all its states. You can make someone like Kyle MacLachlan seem unsympathetic and dull and you can then reverse that. It depends on the trick you want to play. If you're using unfamiliar actors, or actors unfamiliar in a certain role, you have a huge advantage over the audience in that you're not dealing with the clichéd view of the actor. So then you can play wonderful tricks, but you have to know in your own mind, almost in musical terms, how you're going to introduce the characters onto the screen; whether you want to go *pow*! or whether you just want to make a small noise. The minute you see a name actor in what appears to be a minor part, you know immediately that it's not a minor part, it's got to be significant. So you've given the emotional plot away by your casting choices. And, on a certain level, that's the problem with the psychology of a Hollywood film. First, the actor is going to give the plot away, and, second, you have this desire, which comes from some form of insecurity, to tell the audience the entire history of the character in ten minutes. It takes away all the mystery of the character. The joy of making films with virtual unknowns is that one has far more chance of the audience accepting them as believable characters. So, with Nastassja Kinski, even though I know her work, a mainstream American audience doesn't know this woman in the way that they know Jodie Foster or Michelle Pfeiffer.

The film opens quite boldly with Max talking directly to camera to the audience yet, aside from a look later on when he meets his wife at the airport, it's not really carried through except through the occasional voice-over. Why didn't you do more of that?
The truth is that it was only meant to be at the very beginning of the film. The shot at the airport, where he appears to look at the camera, was not designed that way. What actually happened was that in my original script when Max was on the airplane he was still thinking about making love to Karen and was aware that there was the smell of sex about him which his wife would recognize when she picked him up at the airport. He was becoming paranoid about it, smelling his hands, and then there was a shot when he was in the bathroom washing his hands, which pays off later in the finished film when his wife says, 'What's that dreadful smell?' and he goes, 'Cheap cologne from the airplane.' Part of that scenario was an attempt at humour; sitting next to him on the plane was an old woman who was watching him as if she understood exactly what he'd been up to, that he'd been a bad boy. So we shot that scene, but when I cut the film down – unfortunately for her – one of the scenes that hit the floor was the exchange between the two

of them. And when Max got into the car at the airport, the old woman was waiting for a taxi, and as he got into the car she was still staring at him. So the look was actually slightly past camera to this woman. I originally did it without the look, and when I was looking through the dailies and I saw it, I said to myself: it looks like he's looking back at the audience and has suddenly remembered that he had spoken to them earlier, like: 'I can't believe I did that.' There was far more humour in his relationship with the audience than there was with this woman. So I decided to go with that. There is another, very brief moment – again, an accident – when he's having the big fight with his wife after the dinner party where he briefly looks at the camera. I left it in because I liked the fact that he occasionally still referred to the camera. The convention would be that you book-end the film with him talking to the camera at the end, which I find dull. I felt that the narrative was working well enough to pull the audience into the convention of not being acknowledged. I think that if I had ended the film with another direct address to the camera by Max, it would almost be a denial of the emotion that I was trying to make the audience feel about the characters. In other words, you start by inviting the audience into your story and then you get so into it yourself that you forget that you've asked someone to watch. The thing with conventions is to break them or, at least, play with them. And what was helpful about having Max's speech at the beginning is that you can get through a ton of back story in a very short space of time and then get on with the emotional story.

As far as the voice-overs were concerned, the one in the middle allowed me to show him at work on an Armani commercial, which was interesting to make. It was also a gentle attack on the advertising world. Putting voice-over over the commercial meant that the audience wasn't just watching a commercial. Two things were happening at the same time; neither of them were ultimately essential to the film other than as a sort of update of the story. There were other scenes that I dropped that I thought were more laborious, so sometimes one makes a pact with oneself and says, 'Well perhaps voice-over is not the most compelling cinema that I can think of, but it does allow me to cut to the chase.'

What was interesting about the previews in LA was the resistance among the focus groups to Wesley talking to the camera; almost outrage from some people. I know that New Line were also not crazy about the beginning. Eventually, it came down to me cutting an alternative beginning for New Line – but to me, it was so weak. It was just voice-over with Wesley walking, but without him acknowledging the camera. It felt insipid to me. So I said, 'This is a directorial choice – take it or leave it. If you want to take it, take the film.' I felt strongly about it because it weakened the beginning, and if that was the case, then it made me insecure about the film. At that point, New Line said, 'We don't want to have an adversarial relationship with you; we will accept your cut.' So it went through.

You mentioned to me that a critic who had seen the film said to you that he had liked the film but he thought it was a shame that you were forced to have a happy ending.
The 'feel-good factor'. That's the term he used and I was really insulted to hear this, so I responded by saying that the ending was entirely mine and had always been in my mind as the integral point of the story; a sort of non-judgemental ending, if you like. If you're a film-maker who makes a certain kind of film, and you don't deliver that film in the expected shape or form every time – and endings are crucial – then you meet with disappointment in some quarters. For example, if you have a reputation for being a dark film-maker, the clichéd understanding is that you will always deliver an ending in which someone dies tragically, leaving an emotional void somewhere. The last thing I wanted to do was to follow *Leaving Las Vegas* with a reprise of that ending.

Are you worried that an audience might feel that the fact that the two couples are having sex in the same place at the funeral is contrived?
No, I would hope that they would not think that. But as a writer, or as a director, everything you do is a contrivance. In *Leaving Las Vegas*, having Elisabeth Shue turn up in time to have painful, but lyrical, sex with Nic Cage, who dies ten minutes later, is a bit of a contrivance. One could say that it's not very realistic. It is a poetic contrivance. Endings are always a problem and it's human nature that people want a definite closure – whether it's a tragic or happy closure – and I agree with them. You want to get out of a film. It's not like a book that you can have a soft relationship with over a long period of time. The film controls your timing; in a good film

you take the audience on a very strong journey and you want to land in a definite way.

But isn't the ending of One Night Stand *very indefinite in a very definite way? They're together, but the look on their faces is not 'happily ever after'.*
What I tried to do was two things: one, to contrive an ending that has, as it were, a mechanical plot but within that mechanical plot to try at least to be truthful about human nature. There is no such thing as resolution between people, there is merely the ability to move on or stop. So you can kill your characters – which is a far easier way of finishing a film because you leave behind the idea that the train has stopped. But if you want the idea of an ongoing life after the film, then you owe it to a certain kind of audience at least to say, 'There is an element of reality here which is: who knows what's going to happen? We're not too sure that this is going to work either, but we like the characters well enough to hope that it might work out.' For me, I like the idea that you are privileged to drop in on a period of time in something, and at a certain point you're gently shown the door. That's why in *Leaving Las Vegas* Elisabeth Shue's character is so important. She is the ongoing one; Ben is always the terminal one. To introduce a character that was maybe able to carry on as a result of this tragic event was very important to me. The idea that life goes on.

One of the things I wanted to talk about was guilt. Films can often be about rage or grief, but it's quite rare to see a film about guilt. What drew you to that?
It's something I've thought about a lot – for various reasons: family, parents, observing other people. I think it plays a huge part in the way we behave. Allied to this is the fact that Max is in a situation where he is apparently very successful. As Kyle MacLachlan says to him (for the audience's benefit): 'It must be great living out in LA. Do you meet any stars? God, what a life that must be. I envy you.' And you can see from Wesley's face that it's a mixed blessing. As the two combatants say at the dinner party: 'I've seen you kiss ass, you've seen me kiss ass.' There's an absence of self-respect that builds up into a kind of self-loathing for having achieved comfort and wealth through a kind of betrayal of his own art, his own ability. As he says in the beginning of the

film, he was a very successful theatre director. He misses this and you see him trying to put it back into his work. But that's not the same thing: pirating your images, or other people's images, for a commercial is a very debasing thing to do. So by the time we meet him, his entire life is built on a series of personal disappointments. The whole relationship with the Robert Downey character is there to highlight that too.

I thought it was very interesting the way the relationship with the Robert Downey character was interwoven into the relationship between Max and Karen. Musically, for instance. The music in the last moments of Downey's life is associated with Max and Karen finally having sex at the funeral. You get a sense that the physical release between the characters is partly being fuelled by the sense of morality created by Downey's death, and his injunction to Max to seize the moment. I assume the Downey character wasn't in Joe Eszterhas's original script.

No, not even remotely. As I've said, something that I would thank Eszterhas for is this three-act structure – which was like three shopping baskets. It's as if they're three short films with the same characters. I always felt that each act should have the ability to function almost as a separate film; that if you watched them as separate films – after an initial confusion – they should make sense. As far as the third act is concerned, it's always difficult to sort out how you're going to bring your two main characters back together and make a film that isn't just about bringing your two main characters back together. What's interesting about film is that by confusing the audience and building up possibilities, you can involve them more so they are really alert.

So the Downey character brings Max to New York in the first place and serves to bring him and Karen together in the last section, as well as providing the imperative which brings them into each other's arms at the funeral.

In every film I've ever made there are scenes which are immensely personal, but not recognizable to anyone but me. And in this film, for the first time ever, I literally took an autobiographical section and almost word-for-word fed it into the film. The relationship between Wesley and Robert Downey Jr is based on a relationship I had with an American lighting designer who died of AIDS. I was there for the last couple of weeks of his life. I did a drawing of him when he was in hospital. Also, Johanna Torrel, the actress playing the doctor, bears an uncanny resemblance to his doctor. The set was very similar to the look of the Middlesex Hospital where all this took place. So it was a very strange experience to re-create a situation, and then on top of that bring in the Max/Karen relationship. One had a kind of documentary feel versus a fictional world.

Did you feel you were exploiting something in your life as a mechanism to make the plot work?
To me, the real love story in the film is between Wesley and Downey, rather than the no-less-significant one between Wesley and Nastassja . It was good for me to deal with this relationship because in the past I've really concentrated on male–female relationships as being, psychologically, the most dominant that you can have. It allowed the male–female sexual relationship between Nastassja and Wesley to be slightly de-signified. In other words, this wasn't a story of a man being led by his genitals into a bad situation – which perhaps characterized the Truffaut film, which ends darkly – which was presumably the way some critics would have preferred this to end. So the film gives the audience a choice of relationships. There are five relationships going on, and neither one is being given the neon-sign treatment as being the most significant one in the film. So in a sense, one is trying to say: this is a slice of life.

When you say that Wesley isn't being led by his genitals, do you mean that the emotional attachment to Downey is equally as strong as the one to Nastassja? Both can be characterized as 'love'.
The one time that Wesley really emotes in the film is when he breaks down and cries over Robert Downey's hospital bed and they talk about their relationship in a very open way. That allowed me – when I was dealing with the relationship between Wesley and Nastassja – to feel that I didn't have to focus on the erotic elements in quite the same way that one normally does. So when they run into the garden at the funeral wake and start making love, I felt that this scene had to have a strong emotional context. She actually says, 'I missed you so much,' rather than, 'I've got to have you', which is the difference between erotic films and emotional films. Emotional films may use sex as an emotional device; erotic

films use sex as an erotic device full stop. Emotion takes a back seat.

The film is called One Night Stand*, and since the audience knows its implications so well, do you think that they will become impatient about how long it takes Wesley and Nastassja to get into bed? Would it have been better to get it over with sooner so that you could get on with the rest of the story?*
To begin with, the minute I arrived at the casting of Wesley Snipes and Nastassja Kinski, like it or not, you're dealing with two examples of racial stereotyping. So if you put them into bed immediately, you reduce Wesley's character to a sexual cliché; the same with Nastassja's white, blonde character. By reducing it to a sexual encounter, when they meet up a year later all they have in common in that scenario is sex. I therefore made them very deliberately old-fashioned in terms of the way films are made now; for the moment when they really look at one another, when they really connect, I wrote a piece of music which is the most old-fashioned piece of music I've ever written in my life. A piece for piano and strings that is purely a romantic device, which tells the audience that there is a gentleness, an old-fashioned modesty, about the characters. For me it was crucial that the audience cares about them. You're fighting an uphill struggle against a title like *One Night Stand*. It has a hard, nineties sex connotation.

You mention the piece of music you wrote for that moment of recognition between them. Could you say a bit more about the music?
In the past I've always come in fighting for the music, knowing that it would be a struggle, knowing that there would be very aggressive opposition to me doing the score. One always feels a little bit exposed when you're having to fight for something. Say you've been the writer–director and then you're fighting for the score; you can see a look of slight disgust on the executives' faces, like, what is this man's problem? Why doesn't he take the leading role as well? The fact that I started off life as a musician and composer carries absolutely no weight with them because I'm being employed by them as a director and they see the music as an indulgence. Also they would prefer to control the score, because they can do more lucrative deals on soundtracks. So it's always been awkward, but I know that if I'm going to get what I want, I

have to fight for it. But on this film – because I didn't have to fight and had this big, luscious sound to play with – when it came to the mix and the scoring, I had a dialogue with myself. I always hear this voice saying: you shouldn't really need music in a film if the actors are doing their job. Why do you need music to underscore it? And I've always had to deal with that in my mind, because my tendency would be to push the music. And I would think, am I pushing the music because it's the last stage and I'm enjoying it so much? I've got to be aware of that, to pull back. And then at a certain point I felt, no, I believe that music is as important as any other element in a film. What I love about film is its ability not to be naturalistic, and music brings it close to the operatic. I don't like it when the music is there as noise to fill up the soundtrack or because it's a convention. So sometimes I don't use music where I could use music, and at other times when I'm going to use it, I think, I'm not going to be ashamed and reticent about it, I'm going to play it loud. So there are times when even dialogue is drowned by music. It's something that Godard always did and I've admired the way he would completely drown dialogue with music. It will swell and fill everything. I think it's really effective. As with anything in a film, if you're going to do it, you might as well be bold about it.

But what does the writer in you say when the musician in you drowns the carefully worked-out dialogue?
Exactly what the musician says to the writer. There are times when I'll write something which I'll think is a beautiful piece of music – say, where a singer does a beautiful phrase – but when you come to put it into the film, you realize it is important that we hear a particular line of dialogue so you have to take that music down at that point. So the composer part of me has to agree to sacrifice that piece of music. Sometimes the writer has to do that too. In the end, it's all about the final mix. Sometimes you'll have a shot and you'll want to make it very dark and in making that choice you're going to wipe out 70 per cent of the detail in the image. It may have looked more beautiful more brightly exposed, but it's less appropriate. As I get older, as I make more films . . . to me, being less possessive about the elements is crucial. I really don't care about cutting an entire scene now other than the slight

trepidation at making the phone call to the actor saying they're no longer in the film. It's nothing to do with your ability, it's to do with the dynamics of the film.

A FRENCH AFFAIR

The following scene takes place 19 minutes and 45 seconds into François Truffaut's 1981 film, *The Woman Next Door* (*La Femme d'à côté*):

Bernard (Gérard Depardieu) is in a supermarket staring through a hole in a shelf of food. In the background we see Mathilde (Fanny Ardant) slide across into the frame, spot Bernard and decide to come and talk to him. They shop and talk about what an unfortunate coincidence it is that she and her husband have moved into the house next to him (and his wife and small child). How they haven't seen each other for over eight years, since the end of their love affair. How she was unhappy at the time, that she couldn't take any more and walked out of his life. However, they are both older now, mature enough to deal with the situation and also both lucky they have found such great partners. Mathilde thinks that Bernard has a great wife and Bernard feels the same about Mathilde's husband.

We cut to the underground car park, and in a long single take we follow Bernard and Mathilde as they walk and talk their way to the car. Bernard is pushing a trolley of grocery bags. We learn that neither of them has confessed their past relationship to their new partners. They stop for a while and there is a moment when we catch a glimpse of exposed emotion on Mathilde's face as she talks about the pain of their break-up, but she holds it in check and they resume walking. (So far, there has been no music at all on the soundtrack.)

She tells him that he and his wife are invited to dinner next week and she hopes that he will turn up this time (a reference to the fact that he ducked out of the last dinner). 'I'll be there,' he says, 'your faithful servant.' His face has a curious half smile. They have reached the car and she opens the back door and he hands her the bags as she packs them. (The car is unlocked which makes me wonder if this is a comment on the relative safety of France in the early 80s, or the director's decision that it was a lot quicker than having to do the scene fumbling with the car keys.) He watches her with this funny smile as she packs, and when she has finished, he hands her her shoulder bag. (It's difficult to say why exactly, but the way Depardieu does this is rather fine. He is a really interesting actor, and as I write this piece I realize there is no one like him in the British or American acting world.) She takes the bag from him, shuts the back door and they both sort of grin at each other. She says: 'Shall we kiss on it?' (being French, this actually means 'Shall we shake on it?'), and they do a formal double cheek job. She opens the driver's door and faces him (the door is between them). We have by now cut out of the long master shot and are now in a tighter two shot which will hold to the end of the scene. She: 'One more request . . . will you say my name from time to time? I used to know when you were feeling hostile because you'd go a whole day without calling me Mathilde.' He stares at her with the same odd smile as she continues. 'I'm sure you don't even remember.' He looks down and sighs, then looks at her and moves around the car door so they are now next to each other. He puts his right hand onto the side of her face (his hands are huge) and says 'Mathilde'. He says this in a very gentle way. She puts her hand onto his and rubs her face against his hand, then they look at each other, and then they kiss. It's quite a long kiss and, unlike most screen kisses, it's believable. It's the kiss of two ex-lovers who have just realized that the 'ex' is redundant. She eases out of the kiss and her eyes close and she falls to the ground in a dead faint. At this point the music comes in for the first time and it's a very good piece of dramatic, romantic score which really pulls at your heart, especially when Bernard says 'Mathilde' over and over again as he cradles her head in those huge hands. She opens her eyes and he helps her up. She gives him a tragic glance as she gets into the car and starts the engine. He says, 'Sure you can drive?', but she doesn't answer, just floors the accelerator and drives out of the shot leaving Bernard standing alone.

This is a very good film. I've seen it twice now. The first time was at the Phoenix in London and again recently on video. Both times it made me sad (which is good). Let's face it, most films are very boring and vanish quickly from memory.

Wasn't this Truffaut's penultimate film? And wasn't he with the stunning Fanny Ardant at the time? This must have been a tough film for him to make. I think he must have been pretty sad when he shot it. But that is not why the film is so good. The script is very tight, every scene is about one or both of the lovers; the acting is really good and very believable. It's not a sentimental film (and here the sparse use of music is a plus). It's quite erotic but the sex never takes over, it's just something that lovers need to do, they have to have each other. I don't think it's ever funny, but there is a very French scene in which Depardieu cannot get to grips with his car and is very uncool. His job is pretty strange too – he seems to be a driving instructor for supertankers, and we keep seeing him on a scale model of a ship in a scale model of a harbour. It's not the sort of job Tom Cruise would do.

Other reasons why I love this film; it's got so much heart, and it seems to be about *something*. Check it out.

(This appreciation by Mike Figgis of François Truffaut's *The Woman Next Door* originally appeared in *Sight and Sound*.)

One Night Stand was first shown as part of the Official Competition at the Venice Film Festival, September 1997. The cast and crew include:

MAX CARLYLE	Wesley Snipes
KAREN	Natassja Kinski
CHARLIE	Robert Downey Jr
MIMI	Ming-Na Wen
VERNON	Kyle MacLachlan
DON	Thomas Hayden Church
MARGAUX	Amanda Donohoe
GEORGE	Glenn Plummer
PHIL HILL	John Ratzenberger
CHARLIE'S NURSE	Julian Sands
CHARLIE'S FRIEND	Xander Berkely
NATHAN	Vincent Ward

Production Designer	Waldemar Kalinowski
Costume Designer	Enid Harris and Laura Goldsmith
Editor	John Smith
Music by	Mike Figgis
Director of Photography	Declan Quinn
Producer	Annie Stewart
Written and Directed by	Mike Figgis

A Red Mullet Production for New Line Productions Inc.

Note

The following text represents the state of the screenplay as pre-production was about to begin.

One Night Stand

OPENING CREDITS ON BLACK

We hear some beautiful harp music. We hear a man's voice and the credits continue.

MAN'S VOICE-OVER

It was all a dream . . .

(*laughs infectiously*)

. . . no it wasn't. I couldn't resist. Harp music and voice-over at the beginning of a film, as soon as you hear it, it establishes the mood. Personally . . . I start nodding off. I mean, it's a killer . . .

The music changes and goes into a laid-back blues which makes the fingers click. Piano bass and drums with some nice string textures from time to time. The following text should have the feel of an improvised talking blues.

More credits . . .

. . . that's better . . . but sometimes, sometimes voice-over does the trick, which is to give you a lot of information as quickly as possible –

(*speech becomes quicker*)

– information that otherwise would take minutes of valuable screen time. You know . . . those scenes that are just about schematic information where I ask questions and say the character's name and we talk about how long is it since we last saw each other and aren't you the guy that did so and so . . . I'm just saying upfront that this voice-over thing is for your benefit and I'll try to keep it as brief as possible because I've noticed that a lot of films are creeping towards the three-hour mark and there's nothing wrong with ninety minutes . . . Anyway . . . to the point.

Credits continue as we fade up.

EXT. HOTEL IN NEW YORK. AFTERNOON

We follow a man as he walks out of the hotel and into the street. Warm sunlight and lots of people going home in the rush hour. The man is Max, our hero. He's in his mid-thirties and is the kind of man who grows more attractive the more time you spend with him. He's well dressed but in a hip kind of way. The suede jacket is probably Armani.

MAN'S VOICE-OVER

About two years ago I was in New York for the night on business and I arranged to meet my friend Charlie.

CUT TO:

EXT. SUBWAY ENTRANCE. AFTERNOON

Credits continue over slo-mo shot of all the people entering and exiting the subway. We see Max going down the stairs with the crowd.

MAN'S VOICE-OVER

Charlie is gay and recently discovered that he is HIV-positive. We haven't seen each other for five years. I live in LA now but Charlie and I hung out together in New York when I was the most promising theatre director on the Lower East Side and I still think of him as my best friend, even though five years ago we had a big fight over a work thing and haven't spoken since.

CUT TO:

INT. SUBWAY STATION. AFTERNOON

Credits continue . . .

We see Max trying to get on a train and then deciding to wait for the next one. Perhaps he takes out of his shoulder bag a beat-up Leica and maybe he takes a photograph.

MAN'S VOICE-OVER

It was a really stupid fight but pride is a strong thing. I mean . . . he didn't even phone me and tell me he was sick . . . his lover did. I was really nervous about this meeting . . .

CUT TO:

EXT. SUBWAY ENTRANCE. AFTERNOON

Credits continue . . .

Max emerges into the sunlight of the East Village.

MAN'S VOICE-OVER

By the way, my name is Max, I'm married with two kids and I'm thirty-five years old. As I walked to meet Charlie I was thirty-three years old . . . I work in the advertising business, I make commercials. I'm very successful . . . very . . . my commercials win prizes in Europe. Before that I worked with Charlie . . .

EXT. LA MAMA THEATER, EAST 4TH STREET. DAY

We see Max walking down East 4th St. He stops outside the La Mama Theater. He goes in.

CUT TO:

INT. THEATRE. AFTERNOON

Credits start to wind up.

The theatre is dark. A technical light and sound rehearsal is taking place.

Camera is at the back of the stage looking towards the red velvet seats of the auditorium.

In the foreground is a Ballet Dancer, female. To the side, lit by a strobe light, is a Violinist playing a Bach solo.

Taped sounds are heard. A projector flickers, partly lighting the dancer. Other lights come on and off.

Other dancers sit in the red seats and watch. We see Max come in, find a seat and watch, and on his face will be the fact that he is moved by what he sees and that he misses this life.

Final credits . . .

PA VOICE

Thirty minutes, back on stage in thirty.

One of the dancers recognizes Max and turns to say hello. We see Max's POV of the stage. Strange projection of something.

KEVIN

Hey, Max, how's it going in LA, baby?

MAX

Good. How about you?

DANCER

You driving a Porsche? Heard you married a model. Good for you, man. See you later? You around for a while?

Charlie emerges from the lighting booth at the back of the auditorium and walks down the aisle. Charlie is the same age as Max. Already a little thin and greying around the temples. He has a lovely face, a generous smile. He walks past Max and then stops in his tracks, pauses and then turns.

MAX

Really beautiful, Charlie. Better than ever.

CHARLIE

Max!

The two men look at each other. It is clear to Charlie that Max knows.

Ah . . . I told him not to phone you.

MAX

Well . . . I guess he loves you, Charlie. How about a truce?

Big pause.

CHARLIE

How about a cup of coffee.

(*shouts back to his booth*)

Kevin? I'm stepping out for a while. Start repatching everything from four into three and have Billy check circuit twelve. You got that?

KEVIN

Got that, sweetheart. Hey, Max, how's it goin'?

CUT TO:

EXT. OUTDOOR CAFÉ. LATE AFTERNOON

Max and Charlie by a window watching the world go by, drinking cappuccini.

CHARLIE

Everything's fine. Nothing's happened yet. Nothing may happen. No one knows anything.

MAX

How about money . . . medical bills and stuff . . .

CHARLIE

I have good insurance. I don't need your money, Max.

Max looks hurt. Charlie punches him on the arm.

Don't lose your sense of humour, Max. It's good to see you . . . it's great. You look beautiful, baby. And I may need your money . . . I'll let you know . . . if I need to let you know.

MAX

OK . . . You look beautiful too.

Charlie smiles and then so does Max and things are OK.

CHARLIE

Never too late to come out of that closet, baby. How's the family?

MAX

Great. You wanna see photos?

DISSOLVE TO:

INT. LOUNGE OF MAX'S SMART HOTEL, NEW YORK. NIGHT

An interesting space. New money, new design. Attractive waitresses. It's about 10 p.m. and busy. Most of the customers are not from New York: airline people, Eurotrash, media folk. Some banal easy-listening Muzak pushes the noise level up to the acceptable side of loneliness. Cigars are hip and most of the young women are participating. Max is sitting at a table.

With Max are his young assistant, Mickey, eighteen and trendy (maybe she's got a crush on Max), and George, black, somewhere between thirty and forty, short blonde hair (yes, blond). George's sexuality, like that of many of the characters in this story, is ambiguous. He is witty and high-energy.

Last but not least is Margaux, who is thirty-plus and beautiful in an angular, androgynous kind of way. Clothes by Maxfield and a lot of buttons undone on her black shirt. Hair colour of the week, etc. Also fast and funny. Margaux smokes in a quick, nervous manner, always blowing the smoke out of the corner of her mouth, away from anyone who might be offended by it.

The following dialogue is a guide. I'd like it to be improvised if possible.

GEORGE

. . . at least a million, all of the helicopter shots, and Claudia Schiffer, what's her price going to be?

MARGAUX

We don't want Schiffer. She's too white, too English . . .

MICKEY

German, I think she's German.

GEORGE

Shut up, Mickey . . . Whatever, foreign. We should get Cindy, she's American.

MAX

She works with Herb. We should find a new face. Set up a casting call for next month sometime. Let's see everyone.

etc. etc.

As they are talking Margaux looks up and watches someone walking across the room. Max is curious and turns his head just as . . .

Max's POV: an attractive Woman sits down at a table. She seems to be alone.

Back at the table the conversation continues as before. Shop talk, gossip, funny and witty but entirely vacuous. Max listens but is distracted; this is all stuff he's heard before.

He picks up the pack of cigarettes that is on the table, takes a cigarette out. Mickey looks at him. He puts it back into the pack. Meanwhile Margaux and George compete.

Max stares off across the room at the Woman. She is wearing reading glasses and working on a pile of papers while she eats.

Max takes out his Leica and takes a frame or two without looking through the viewfinder.

Angle – she looks up and for a moment their eyes meet but she quickly looks down again and continues working.

Max looks at his watch. He starts to get up.

What's check-out tomorrow?

MICKEY

Twelve. We have to be at the airport by two and there's the UN celebrations starting and the traffic is going to be very bad. Are you going to bed now?

MAX

Yeah, I'm beat.

MICKEY

I'm tired as well. Goodnight, everyone.

GEORGE

Don't go to bed, it's boring. We're going to the Bowery bar. You said you'd be there.

MARGAUX

Let him go to bed. Goodnight . . . goodnight.

Max walks out of the bar, followed by Mickey, who is trying to act casual but is in fact hoping to go to bed with Max.

MICKEY

Don't you love the architecture of this place? Is that Christian Slater?

(*spots someone she knows*)

Oh, hi, how are you? Bye, bye.

As Max passes the Woman he glances down but she doesn't look up, being engrossed in her work.

CUT TO:

INT. HOTEL CORRIDORS. NIGHT

Max and Mickey step out of the elevator. Max stops outside his room and fits the key. Mickey stops also. Max opens the door, kisses Mickey on the cheek, steps into his room and closes the door. Mickey hangs for a moment and then walks away whistling.

INT. MAX'S HOTEL ROOM. NIGHT

Max flicks through the channels on TV as he picks up the phone and dials a number. MTV, hotel porn, talk shows, etc. He walks to the window with the phone and looks out on the night skyline of Manhattan.

MAX

Hi, it's me . . . I should be back by five tomorrow . . . Miss you all . . . Big kiss and a hug . . . See you then.

CUT TO:

INT. HELICOPTER. NEW YORK CITY. MORNING

Traffic newscaster announces huge traffic problems for the city today.

INT. HOTEL LOBBY. MORNING

Max is checking out. The lobby is busy with people checking in. Lots of security and foreign-looking men of all nationalities. He signs his AmEx form. The clerk is possibly English. Max has a big shoulder bag.

MAX

Really busy today . . . What's going on?

CLERK

UN celebrations. It's a joke, every room is booked. Hope they all don't decide to go shopping at the same time. Leave for the airport early, sir. It's a madhouse out there.

Max looks at his watch.

MAX

Maybe you should ring my friends . . . 905, 906 and 907 . . . Thanks.

INT. HOTEL LOBBY (LATER). DAY

Max sitting at a table in the lobby, briefcase open. He writes something with an antique fountain pen, then caps the pen and puts it in his inside jacket pocket. We see the attractive Woman sitting behind Max. Max does not see her at first.

She is having a meeting with a group of suits, men and women. Some of them are Italian, some are German, some are French. She seems equally at ease in all the languages.

INT. HOTEL LOBBY (LATER). DAY

Max reading the New York Times *and drinking a cup of coffee. He looks up and sees the attractive Woman. He stands up, stretches and sits down again, this time in the seat opposite her. He carries on with his newspaper, glancing at her from time to time.*

Angle – the Woman. The meeting comes to an end and one of the men leaves after shaking her hand. She sits and gathers her papers and finishes her coffee.

Angle – Max. He puts down his paper, finishes his coffee and rubs his eyes. He glances over at . . .

Angle – the Woman. She is staring at him. She gets up and walks over to him, sits opposite him.

WOMAN

You have a black heart!

MAX

Excuse me?

WOMAN

I think maybe your pen . . .

She points at his heart. Max looks down. There is a black stain on his shirt. He sits up carefully and opens his jacket. The lining is also black with ink.

Oh my goodness.

He carefully opens his jacket and takes the fountain pen out of the inside pocket. The cap has come off. Max stands there feeling more than foolish and uncool holding the jacket away from the shirt.

Don't move.

She goes to the bar and comes back with some napkins. People are staring at them curiously. The napkins are put to work and much of the black mess is absorbed . . . but Max is not looking exactly suave.

Maybe you should change for lunch.

MAX

I checked out of my room already.

They look in the direction of the check-in.

Angle – check-in desk. Chaos as about fifty people wait to get their rooms.

CUT TO:

INT. HOTEL ELEVATOR. DAY

Max and the Woman are crunched together in a very full elevator (most of the nations of the world are represented), Max still holding the jacket away from the shirt, his leather bag over his shoulder. They speak quietly, as one does in an elevator.

WOMAN

Karen.

MAX

Max. Nice to meet you, Karen.

And they shake hands, which makes them both smile. The doors to the elevator open and they both get out.

CUT TO:

INT. KAREN'S HOTEL SUITE. DAY

They come into the room. It's the same as Max's suite only with different art on the wall. The room is on the top floor of the building and the view of the city is spectacular. She opens the bathroom door.

MAX

Listen . . . thank you for this. I'll be really quick. I'm not usually this gauche.

KAREN

I believe you.

The phone rings.

Help yourself . . . Excuse me.

She walks to the other room and picks it up.

Hello? Oh, hi . . . We still on for tonight?

Max goes into the bathroom with his bag and closes the door quietly.

CUT TO:

INT. BATHROOM. DAY

Max takes his jacket and shirt off. His chest is stained with the ink. He looks for a plastic laundry bag, finds one, puts his shirt in it. Thinks about it and then dumps the bag in the trash. Tries to wash some of the ink off his chest. Opens his overnight bag and takes out a dirty shirt, sniffs the armpits and puts it on. As he is buttoning it he looks around and sees her lingerie drying on a radiator. He notices that he has knocked a pair of her panties on to the floor. He picks them up and looks at them, puts them back carefully.

CUT TO:

INT. KAREN'S HOTEL SUITE. DAY

Max comes out of the bathroom. Karen is just hanging up the phone. She looks annoyed.

MAX

Thank you so much. This was very kind of you, thank you.

She walks to the door with him. Opens it.

Are you all right? Not bad news or anything?

KAREN

That was my girlfriend. We were going to a concert tonight and now she can't make it.

MAX

That's too bad. What was the concert?

KAREN

Oh, heavy stuff, string quartets.

MAX

Quartetto Italiano?

This impresses her. She puts her head on one side and re-evaluates him. Max savours his little moment for a while longer and then owns up.

There's a review in the *Times* this morning . . .

(*beat*)

. . . and I saw the tickets as we came in . . . on the table.

KAREN

And you like the Quartetto Italiano?

Her accent is a lot better than Max's.

MAX

I just bought the late Beethoven series on CD. My records were worn thin. They're brilliant. I tried for tickets but they were sold out. I'm jealous. You'll still go?

KAREN

Oh yes. I'm sure I can sell the other ticket . . . anyway . . .

There is a pause, awkward but nice.

I guess you're leaving town, right?

MAX

(*looking at his watch*)

On my way right now. Well . . . really nice to have met you.

KAREN

You too.

MAX

Oh, by the way, I dumped my shirt in your waste basket.

KAREN

That'll give the maid something to talk about.

Max looks at her mouth. Her lips are soft and slightly moist.

Image – the two of them facing each other. A second image of them is superimposed in which Karen reaches up and kisses Max on the mouth. This second image is much fainter than the real image and it is in black and white. It retreats into the real image and fades away, leaving the two of them staring at each other. Max offers her his hand to shake. She takes it.

MAX

Bye.

KAREN

Goodbye.

She goes inside and closes the door. Max stares at it.

Angle – the door. The room number is 50101. Max walks away whistling.

CUT TO:

INT. LOBBY OF THE HOTEL. DAY

We see George, Margaux and Mickey running across the lobby with their bags, George and Margaux looking the worse for wear and Mickey looking for Max. She wants to hang on but the other two grab her and hustle her out of the door to a waiting limo.

Angle – Max arrives in the lobby and looks around for them. He looks at his watch and then walks to the desk, which is busier than ever. He pushes in to the front of the line and speaks to the desk clerk.

Max rushes out of the hotel.

CUT TO:

EXT. HOTEL. DAY

Max rushes out of his hotel into a taxi.

INT. TAXI. DAY

Max takes a taxi to the airport.

EXT. NEW YORK STREETS. DAY

Gridlock. A demo is taking place. Hundreds of yellow cabs not going anywhere in a hurry. Stretch limos with escorts. A Dixieland band playing something funky. A marching band playing something else. Bagpipes, etc., etc. Cops everywhere (this was the most expensive scene in the film).

Angle – yellow cab. Max gets out of a cab, pays the driver and walks away.

CUT TO:

INT. HELICOPTER. NEW YORK CITY. AFTERNOON

Traffic newscaster describes huge gridlock below.

EXT. STREET PAYPHONE. AFTERNOON

MAX

(*voice-over*)

Hey, it's Max and I've missed my flight. I'm booked on the first one tomorrow, gets in about 11 a.m. I'm not at the hotel any more, they're booked out, it's hard to get a room anywhere. Think I'll just head out for the airport this evening and wait for the flight. See you all tomorrow. Hope you all had a nice time with Gran and Gramps.

Max hangs up, looks at the phone, picks it up again, puts quarters in, begins to dial and then hangs up.

CUT TO:

EXT. FERRY TO ELLIS ISLAND. AFTERNOON

Max looks at the architecture. He looks up high.

MAX

(*voice-over*)

I didn't miss the plane on purpose, but I did know that I was supposed to miss it. It crossed my mind that maybe it was going to crash . . . but I didn't think so, not with George on board. In all the time that I had spent in New York, I'd never been up the Twin Towers.

INT. ELLIS ISLAND. AFTERNOON

Max is a tourist.

He walks around looking at the view of the city, takes a photograph or two perhaps, looks at his watch, heads for the elevator, passes a payphone and hesitates. He looks at a payphone and the payphone looks at him. He picks up the phone and dials.

MAX

Hello . . . room 50101, please.

CUT TO:

EXT. SMALL RECITAL ROOMS. DUSK

Crowds of people milling about in evening dress. Max (still in his Armani grunge) searches the crowd and then sees . . . Karen. She smiles a big smile when she sees him.

He's grinning like a loon as they say hello. She looks very attractive. Now they are both embarrassed and don't know what to say next. They enter the theatre.

INT. THEATRE STAIRCASE. EVENING

Karen and Max walk up the staircase. They both speak at the same time.

KAREN

No, you go first.

MAX

I just wanted to say . . . upfront . . . that I'm not trying to pick you up and . . . thanks for the ticket.

KAREN

Maybe I should be offended.

They both laugh.

It's all right, I know you're a gentleman. And I know you're married.

(*holds up her left hand*)

Snap! Thank you for being my escort. I'd decided not to go.

MAX

I'm not dressed for this.

Max is getting some strange looks.

KAREN

You're fine . . . So what happened with your flight?

MAX

Traffic was so bad . . .

And they go into the hall with the crowd.

CUT TO:

INT. RECITAL ROOMS. NIGHT

The music is breathtaking. A middle quartet. And we listen to it for a while and watch the players.

Karen and Max have very good seats, first row of the balcony, the quartet very close to them. Karen sits forward, her elbows on the rail, her head in her hands, engrossed in the music. Max looks at her, fascinated.

Without her coat she looks attractive and mysterious in cashmere and pearls.

Angle – Max's POV. Karen is beautiful. The camera goes tight into her half-profile, her head moving slightly to the music. Her hair is up and the back of her neck has a peach fuzz that is very attractive.

Angle – fantasy image. We see, in monochrome, Max's hand reach out and the fingers go into her hair and pull her head back gently. Then we mix back to reality. (It has to be clear that this is not actually happening.) In the background we can see the string quartet playing.

Angle – Karen. She half turns and looks at Max, holds the look for quite a while and then smiles. There is a lot in the smile. Some insecurity, some warmth. It makes her seem very young.

CUT TO:

INT. BAR IN RECITAL ROOMS. NIGHT

On long lens we see Max and Karen talking animatedly in the jam of people next to the bar (but we don't hear the conversation). Another man says hello to Karen and glances at Max. Karen finishes saying hello to him and turns back to Max. All the sound drains from the scene as we zoom in on Max listening to something Karen is telling him. We hear the music from . . .

CUT TO:

INT. RECITAL ROOMS. NIGHT

. . . the quartet, who are now playing the slow movement from String Quartet No. 13 in B flat (Cavatina, adagio molto expressivo), *arguably one of the most emotional pieces of music ever written. The*

camera cuts between Max and Karen, both a little misty-eyed with the music. Max leans forward and puts his head on his hands. Karen looks at him.

Angle – Karen's POV of Max. He's a sexy man. Broad shoulders, strong but not too over-developed. Nice hands.

Fantasy image – monochome. She takes his hand and places it on her breast.

Back to reality. Max turns and looks at her and then leans in to her ear and says something. She nods and they both look back to the quartet on stage.

Angle – the stage. The quartet finish the movement.

CUT TO:

INT. RECITAL ROOMS. NIGHT

The concert has ended. Max and Karen walk down the stairway.

KAREN

What did you think?

MAX

I thought it was . . . really beautiful. Thank you. Did you enjoy it?

KAREN

Oh, very much. Thank you for coming. It would have been a shame to miss it.

And they both look around and think about the next move a while.

I'm hungry. Are you hungry?

MAX

Yeah. Let's find something to eat.

KAREN

Well, only if you have time. Do you . . .?

MAX

I have plenty of time.

KAREN

(*looks at her watch*)

It's quite late.

CUT TO:

INT. TAXI. NIGHT

Wild taxi ride.

CUT TO:

INT. A FUNKY BAR. NIGHT

They're talking, eating, and having the nicest time. We may hear what they are saying but probably not – this is a loud, friendly bar. Great music on the juke box, nice and loud. They drink wine and order another half-bottle. The music finishes. Karen goes to the bathroom.

Max goes over to the juke box and selects. We hear something really good, like 'Making Whoopee' by Ray Charles. Karen comes over to the juke. The wine has mellowed her.

KAREN

This is very nice.

MAX

You like it?

KAREN

Of course I like it. It's a great piece of music. Why wouldn't I like it? What is this . . . a test?

MAX

Maybe . . . You choose something.

KAREN

Fine . . . fine. You do realize that this could be a history-changing moment. You obviously had me figured as a purist. OK, sit down and let me think about this.

They are both smiling but also aware that it is not entirely a joke. Max sits down and Karen studies the selection.

Angle – close-up on the juke. Karen makes her choice and walks away.

Angle – Karen and Max at the table.

Music kicks in. Nina Simone – 'My Baby Just Cares for Me' (or something equally good and available to us!).

MAX

Pretty good.

Karen takes some cigarettes from her bag.

KAREN

Do you mind?

MAX

No . . . Can I have one?

KAREN

Sure. I think we have to go outside.

They step out to the entrance. Max lights up for both of them and suddenly they find themselves looking into each other's eyes for a beat.

So . . . did you check into another hotel?

MAX

No, it wasn't worth it. My flight is early.

KAREN

So what are you going to do?

MAX

I'm going to take a cab out to JFK in a while and wait there.

They both become a little uncomfortable. The evening is coming to an end and they are not going to be bad because they are both responsible people. But sometimes it is very difficult to deny the attraction two people feel for each other. The Barman comes out to where they are standing.

BARMAN

I'm sorry, there's no smoking here. You have to go on to the street.

They stub out the cigarettes. The Nina Simone track finishes and Karen glances at her watch.

MAX

What time is it?

KAREN

(*regretfully*)

One.

MAX

I'll walk you back.

A beat.

KAREN

OK. Thanks. This was very nice, thank you.

CUT TO:

EXT. A QUIET STREET BETWEEN TWO BUSY AVENUES. NIGHT

Max has his shoulder bag with him. As they get closer to the camera we pick up on their conversation.

MAX

. . . I studied piano until I was eighteen, then I had to choose between art or commerce and . . . commerce won.

KAREN

Do you regret it?

MAX

No.

(*beat*)

Sure. Whenever I see something, hear something like tonight . . . I regret it, but I never would have been that good. I worked in theatre for a while.

KAREN

But do you still play?

MAX

My piano is still at my parents' house. We don't have room for it. Do you play?

KAREN

Cello, at school. I still have it.

MAX

Where were you born?

KAREN

Aha, you hear my accent . . .

Two young white men are walking behind them, gaining on them. Max becomes aware of them at the last moment and takes Karen's arm to guide her to one side of the path so that the others can overtake. She is explaining something about her parents being European and travelling around a lot when she was a child . . .

Events move quickly. They are in a dark area between two streetlights. One of the men starts to overtake them and he indicates to them that he would like a light for his cigarette. Max suddenly realizes that things are not quite right. A knife is pulled on him and the other man grabs Karen from behind, his arm around her throat.

1ST MUGGER

Give me your wallet. Hurry up.

Max is very alert and calm. The muggers have English accents.

MAX

OK, take it easy. You can have money . . . Take it easy . . .

Max moves slowly . . . carefully watching the guy who has Karen in a throat hold.

2ND MUGGER

Take off your watch. Hurry . . .

Karen takes off her watch. The guy snatches it and yanks open her coat, see the pearls.

MAX

Hey now . . . take it easy. You can have money. Look, I have money.

And Max pulls out some notes to show them.

2ND MUGGER

. . . the beads, lady. Take them off.

Karen looks at Max. Across the street a couple walk along in animated conversation, unaware of what is taking place. Karen tries to play for time.

KAREN

They were my mother's.

2ND MUGGER

Take 'em off . . . or he'll cut 'em off.

MAX

It's OK. Do as he says.

The couple walk away and the moment is gone.

Angle – Karen's, Max's POV. Pearls are not easy to take off. Karen reaches behind her neck to unfasten the safety catch.

The Mugger puts his free hand on her breasts.

2ND MUGGER

Very nice.

Max goes very still and quiet.

MAX

Don't do that, man. Just take the stuff and get the fuck out of here.

1ST MUGGER

Shut your face. Maybe we'll fuck your wife for you. Probably been a while since you got it up.

Karen tries to move out of the 2nd Mugger's grip. He grabs her hair and pulls her back in line, his hand even tighter on her breast. She gives a small cry of pain.

Angle – on Max. His face transforms. He becomes caveman. He becomes killer. He loses control and goes for the 1st Mugger. It's dark and we see the knife flash and then a high-pitched scream as Max's knee connects with testicles. The guy drops to his knees and the knife is kicked from his hand. Max picks it up and turns on 2nd Mugger, who still has a hold on Karen and is trying to drag her to one side. Max gets behind him, with the knife to his throat. Rage and adrenalin have turned him into a formidable sight.

MAX

(*whispering*)

OK . . . listen up carefully now. One false move and . . .

(*shouts*)

I'm going to cut off your fucking head . . . Understand? UNDERSTAND?

2ND MUGGER

Understand, man. Easy with that thing.

MAX

Right . . . first you're going to let go of the lady . . .

He lets go of Karen, who backs away from him. Her pearls fall to the ground.

It's a weird situation, because there is not a lot that Max can do with just one knife except kill the guy, and he's not that far gone. The other Mugger is starting to get up, moaning low and with his hand between his legs. Karen moves to behind Max and holds on to his arm. Max improvises as his grasp on reality returns.

. . . and then you're going to apologize to her for what you just did . . .

(*shouts*)

Say it!

2ND MUGGER

Lady, I'm real sorry.

MAX

Then you and your friend are . . . going with me . . . yes . . . that's it . . . to talk to the cops . . .

1ST MUGGER

(*high-pitched groan*)

Fuck that.

And 1st Mugger gets up and staggers off into the darkness.

2ND MUGGER

(*close to tears*)

Hey . . . Jonathan . . . wait.

Max takes the knife away from his throat and allows him to run off after his friend. There's not a lot more he can do. He puts an arm around Karen.

MAX

You OK?

KAREN

Yes. Let's get out of here.

Max picks up his wallet and her pearls, folds up the knife and puts it in his pocket. Then he grabs her hand and they walk off and then run. Camera tracks with them in and out of the pools of light towards the bright avenue.

CUT TO:

EXT. BRIGHT AVENUE. NIGHT

They emerge, out of breath, into the busy avenue, thick with traffic. As they cross the street Max puts his arm around her protectively. A group of cops is talking next to a squad car. They both have the same thought.

MAX

Do you want to report it?

Sure, but if they go to the police . . . it could be awkward. And it will take hours. They look at each other and she shakes her head. But they are still very shaken by what happened. As they walk off she reaches for his hand.

CUT TO:

EXT. HOTEL. NIGHT

Taxi pulls up outside hotel.

INT. TAXI AT HOTEL. NIGHT

KAREN

You're a brave man, Max.

MAX

No, I was very stupid . . . Could have got you killed. Will you be all right?

KAREN

Yeah . . . in a while. I'm still a bit . . . you know . . . I think my heart must be beating very fast.

MAX

You want to go bed? I mean . . . you know what I mean . . .

KAREN

Yes, I know . . . No . . . not yet.

MAX

Would you like me to stay with you for a while? We could sit in the lobby.

KAREN

OK.

EXT. HOTEL. NIGHT

Max and Karen exit the cab and enter the hotel.

INT. HOTEL LOBBY. NIGHT

They walk through the lobby. Cleaning staff are at work with vacuum cleaners and the noise is not so nice. Without saying anything, Karen walks to the elevators. Max hangs back a little but as the doors open she looks at him and they both get in.

CUT TO:

INT. HOTEL ROOM. NIGHT

The light comes on in Karen's room and she and Max enter. She goes straight to the mini-bar and pours the two of them brandies. They clink glasses.

MAX

Here's to life.

KAREN

To life.

They drink.

I like the name Max . . . It suits you.

MAX

Yep.

(*laughs*)

Karen's nice too.

Max looks at his glass and thinks about making the brandy last a little longer. He drains it in one and stands up.

KAREN

What time do you have to be at JFK?

MAX

Eight.

KAREN

OK. Take the other bed. I'll set the alarm for six-thirty.

MAX

It's OK . . . really. I'm gonna go now.

KAREN

Where? Where are you going to go?

MAX

JFK.

Karen takes a cigarette and lights it. Her hands are a little shaky.

KAREN

Listen, you just saved my life, we're both adult, we're both married. It's the least I can do. I want to use the bathroom first. OK? Settled?

Silence. It gets very quiet in the room. Close-up on Karen.

Listen . . . I'd like you to stay.

MAX

OK . . . settled.

CUT TO:

INT. HOTEL BEDROOM. NIGHT

Max comes into the bedroom in a T-shirt and jockey shorts. Karen is already curled up and seems to be sleeping. He gets into his bed and . . .

KAREN

(*sleepy*)

I set the alarm . . . See you in the morning. Goodnight.

MAX

Goodnight. Thanks.

He turns off the bedside light. They both have their backs to each other.

Angle – Max's face.

Angle – Karen's face.

FADE TO BLACK.

FADE UP TO:

INT. BEDROOM (LATER). NIGHT

The curtains are open, showing the city at night. Max is awake but lying on his side, facing the wall. Behind him we see Karen sitting up. She gets out of bed and goes out of the room, comes back with some water, gets back into her bed. We hear little sobs. She is genuinely trying to hold the noise down.

MAX

You all right?

She says nothing but the shaking gets more pronounced and then she is crying but trying to hold it all back.

Hey . . . hey. You want to come here?

She gets into bed with Max. He puts his arms around her and she lets go of her emotion.

There, there . . . It's OK, it's all OK.

He rubs her back for a while and she calms down gradually. His hands make their way into hair and he massages her scalp and pulls the hair gently. She gives an involuntary moan.

Does that hurt?

KAREN

No . . .

(*sniff*)

I think you'd better stop.

Max stops and they lie still for a moment and then she starts to get out of the bed to return to her own.

Thank you . . . Sorry.

Max puts his hand on her arm to stop her.

Max.

MAX

What?

KAREN

I think I should get into my own bed again.

(*beat*)

Shouldn't I?

Max lets go of her arm.

MAX

Yeah . . . you should.

KAREN

Would you like me to massage your shoulders?

MAX

Yes . . . I would like.

KAREN

OK . . . sit up straight.

Max does as he is told and she works on him for a while. His head drops down to his chest. She is very good, finds a knot and works it. The pain is divine; her hands are very strong. She pulls up his T-shirt and takes it over his head.

And then she kisses him on his back. Very tender and gentle. She kisses him again and works her way around his body until they are facing each other. Max undoes the buttons to her nightdress and very slowly exposes a breast. He gazes at it as if it were a work of art. Karen also looks at it.

He really hurt me.

Max gently cups her breast with his hand and watches as her nipple hardens.

MAX

Yeah. It's interesting, I had to stop myself from killing him.

He kisses the nipple and then looks into her eyes.

They are incredibly beautiful.

KAREN

You don't think they're too small?

MAX

No, they're perfect. I've wanted to kiss them all night.

KAREN

Oh, really.

MAX

Yes, really.

Max gently reveals her other breast. He goes to kiss it and then stops.

You want me to?

KAREN

No.

MAX

OK.

KAREN

I want you to kiss me on my mouth.

And he does. They have to decide now whether this is going to turn into something else. She puts her hands on his head and breaks the kiss and creates a little distance. They regard each other seriously.

Max?

MAX

I know . . . OK . . . You're right.

He buttons up her nightdress and lies down, pulling her into the cradle of his arm. She resists for a beat and then settles with him.

What a crazy day.

KAREN

Yeah.

MAX

But a nice day.

KAREN

Yes.

MAX

Goodnight, Karen.

KAREN

Goodnight, Max.

FADE TO BLACK.

FADE UP TO:

INT. BEDROOM. EARLY DAWN

Faint light is now coming from the window. The city looks incredible. The tops of the skyscrapers are hidden in cloud. Max wakes and looks at his watch. 4 a.m.

He turns to see if Karen is awake. She is asleep, lying on her back, her left leg bent and away from her body, the sheet covering her legs. Max lifts the sheet carefully until he can see her body. Her nightdress has ridden up, exposing the white triangle of her panties. Max gently strokes her inner thighs with the back of his fingers. Her legs part slightly. He touches her between her legs. She sighs and turns on to her side, into Max. She wakes for a moment and opens her eyes . . . for a moment she is startled and then she remembers and smiles.

KAREN

Hi . . .

. . . before snuggling in tight to him and then going back to sleep.

FADE TO BLACK.

FADE UP TO:

INT. BEDROOM. DAWN

Camera tight on Max as he wakes up in a state of deep arousal. Karen is kissing his neck and then she moves to his mouth. Camera pulls back and we see that they are under a sheet. Karen has her hand on his penis. He puts his hand between her legs. They're kissing each other very gently.

This is a love scene, not a sex scene. The emphasis is on the emotion rather than the nudity or any perverse voyeuristic elements.

I think maybe I'd like to throw this out of focus in the foreground and be sharp on the city through the window. The lovers would be close to camera and intimate but out of focus. Also, it is still pretty dark in the room.

Max kisses her neck and then slowly makes his way down her body, pulling up her nightdress, kissing her breasts and then her stomach. Her hands are in his hair, massaging his head.

MAX

Do you believe in love at first sight?

KAREN

Max . . . Shut up.

Max moves down to her white panties and kisses her thighs and then the triangle.

MAX

Open your legs.

She does. Max puts his hand inside her panties and them moves back up to kiss her mouth. The sexuality is in the kiss.

I love it that you're so wet.

KAREN

Yes? I'm embarrassed.

MAX

Don't be.

KAREN

OK.

She sits up, pushes Max on to his back and looks down at his body. The camera is low, looking up at her.

You're very beautiful, Max.

She leans down, just out of frame, to suck him for a while. Max plays with her breasts and sits up to watch her, strokes her back. He puts his fingers inside her panties.

MAX

Take these off?

KAREN

All right.

She helps him and then climbs on top of him, puts him inside her, then begins moving on him.

MAX

No . . . keep still. Don't move.

So they try and keep very still, which is difficult because it goes against every instinct. They kiss and look at each other and Max plays with her breasts.

But he doesn't grab them and squeeze them and all that stuff. He cups them with his hands, trying not to touch them, just brushing them. They are completely aroused now.

She takes his hand and kisses. it. Sucks the fingers.

KAREN

Look . . . he cut you. I'll heal it for you.

She kisses the cut.

MAX

I could come any second now. What should I do?

KAREN

What do you mean, Max?

MAX

Should I come in you?

KAREN

Or on me, Max? Is that what you mean?

Max laughs.

What's funny, Max?

MAX

You are . . . Karen. Do you know how wonderful it is to make love with you?

KAREN

Yes, I do, I know my own worth, I have very high self . . . esteem . . . Max, oh fuck, Max, I'm going to come.

MAX

Then you'd better answer my question. I mean quickly.

KAREN

Lie to me, Max. Tell me you love me, say my name.

MAX

OK . . . Tell me when.

KAREN

Now . . . now!

MAX

I love you.

KAREN

Say my name, Max, say my name.

MAX

Karen . . . I love you, Karen, OK?

KAREN

Oh God, Max. Say it again, Max.

MAX

No . . . you tell me.

KAREN

You want me to lie to you as well, Max?

MAX

That's right.

As they both come . . .

KAREN

I love you, Max. I love you . . . Max . . .

FADE TO BLACK.

FADE UP:

INT. BEDROOM. DAWN

Max and Karen asleep under a sheet, entwined in each other, her hand on his penis, his hand between her legs.

Angle – the alarm clock says 6.30. It goes off with a deafening ring.

CUT TO:

EXT. SKY. DAY

A big passenger jet appears like magic out of a dense bank of cloud.

CUT TO:

INT. PLANE. DAY

Max looking out of the window down at the clouds. Camera moves in tight on his face, which is expressionless.

CUT TO:

FLASHBACK: INT. HOTEL. DAWN

His hand on Karen's breast. Her face looking down at him.

CUT TO:

EXT. LANDSCAPE. DAY

Midwestern landscape seen from 32,000 feet. Scattered clouds.

CUT TO:

INT. PLANE. DAY

Max, nursing a Scotch, rocks, brings his fingers to his nose. He can still smell her. He kisses his own hand.

CUT TO:

FLASHBACK: INT. RECITAL ROOMS. THE NIGHT BEFORE

Karen leaning forward . . . her neck . . . his hand in her hair . . . turning to look at him . . . smiling.

BACK TO:

INT. PLANE. DAY

Max strokes his lips with his fingers and then notices the Old Lady sitting next to him, who has clearly been watching him for some time. Max looks out of the window.

CUT TO:

EXT. LANDSCAPE. DAY

The desert around Las Vegas seen from 32,000 feet.

ANNOUNCEMENT
(*voice-over*)
. . . will be landing at Los Angeles international airport in approximately 45 minutes . . .

CUT TO:

INT. PLANE TOILET. DAY

Max is washing his hands and face and applying a liberal amount of cologne.

CUT TO:

INT. LAX ARRIVALS. DAY

People waiting for people. Camera searches the faces. We see a woman, a bit careworn and miserable, angrily looking at her watch. Is this Max's wife?

Angle – another woman, quite interesting-looking but very plain. Could this be her? She looks bookish.

Angle – arrivals board. New York flight has landed.

Angle – another woman. This one seems more likely. More of a homely type.

Angle – the gate. Max comes through with his bag. He scans the faces. Doesn't see who he is expecting to see. Walks on out to the exterior door and exits to the street.

EXT. AIRPORT PICK-UP ZONE. DAY

Max looks around. We hear a car horn hooting. A pink Jeep Cherokee pulls up with a screech of brakes. The driver is a stunning blonde. This is his wife, Mimi. Mimi looks to be about thirty, with blonde hair and a body that any woman would be envious of. She is wearing a very short skirt and a tight tank top. Her breasts are contained in a sports bra and as she jumps out of the Cherokee a passing car almost collides with a taxi and there is much honking of horns. Mimi hugs Max and lifts her feet off the ground so that he has to take her weight for a moment. It's the sort of pose that you see a lot in commercials. Max feels his back start to go and pats her bottom to let her know she should take her weight back on to her own feet.

MIMI

Maximilian . . . we've missed you. Bad boy staying that extra night.

MAX

(*looking around*)

Where are the kids?

MIMI

Next door with Janie. I wanted to come all by myself. Did you miss me?

MAX

(*kissing her*)

Of course I missed you, honey.

She kisses him open-mouthed and quickly darts her tongue between his lips. Over her shoulder Max notices the Old Lady who was sitting next to him passing and eyeing him curiously.

Angle – the Old Lady. She winks at Max. Somehow this is shocking.

Max disentangles himself, picks up his bag, walks to the back of the Cherokee and opens the tailgate.

You want me to drive?

MIMI

Sure.

CUT TO:

INT. CHEROKEE. CENTURY BOULEVARD. DAY

Mimi suddenly puts her hand on his crotch and squeezes hard.

MIMI

Grrrrr . . . tiger!

The car does a mini-swerve. Much horn-hooting and finger-fucking gestures from other drivers.

MAX

You gotta warn me if you're going to do that, honey.

MIMI

Whoops. Sorry. It's just a way of saying how much I missed you. Did you miss me?

MAX

Of course I did. How was it with Gramps?

MIMI

It was fine. What's that smell?

MAX

What smell?

Mimi comes in close and nuzzles his neck.

MIMI

That smell.

MAX

Oh, that smell. Cologne from the plane. Cheap shower substitute.

MIMI

Poor Max. It must have been awful not having a bed to sleep in.

MAX

It was OK . . . but I should sleep well tonight.

MIMI

(*laughing*)

I wouldn't bank on it, honey.

CUT TO:

EXT. HOUSE IN THE BURBS. DAY

Two children and a big dog (Oscar) come running out to greet Max as the Cherokee pulls up. Branford is eight and Safron is ten. Safron gets first hug, Branford holds back until Max goes to him. He is quite shy and withdrawn.

MAX

Hey, Branflakes, how about a kiss for Daddy?

Max gives him a disgusting wet kiss, blows a raspberry on his neck until he is giggling helplessly, pleading for mercy. Safron is enjoying the spectacle immensely until Max turns and stares at her like a lunatic. He lunges out and tries to grab her and she runs into the house, giggling and screaming, followed by the boys.

Come on, let's kiss her to death.

BRANFORD

Yes . . . let's get her.

CUT TO:

INT. HOUSE. EVENING

The four of them having supper. It's take-out Chinese.

MAX

Mmmm . . . this is delicious.

MIMI

It's from the new place in the mall. Janie told me about it so I thought tonight was special . . . and . . .

MAX

Thank you. Mummy is a very thoughtful person, isn't she, kids?

BRANFORD

What's thoughtful?

SAFRON

Full of thought, dumbo.

Branford aims a punch at his sister's arm. Max catches his hand.

MAX

Hey, no violence towards women.

Mimi puts her hand on to Max's.

MIMI

You're going to think I'm stupid, but last night, after I got your message, I couldn't stop thinking about New York and how violent it is . . . I had this image of you being mugged.

Max squeezes her hand.

MAX

And here I am, safe and sound.

The dog comes up to Max and starts sniffing. She won't go away.

Come on, Oscar, I'm trying to eat supper.

Max tries to move the dog away but she keeps sniffing and does a little growl. The kids laugh.

MIMI

Oscar, what can you smell on Daddy?

MAX

I guess he doesn't like the cologne either.

MIMI

The dog has taste, Max.

BRANFORD

I like it . . . a lot. What is colome anyhow?

Max is starting to sweat a little. He pushes his plate away.

MAX

Okey-dokey, I can take a hint. Daddy is going to take a shower.

Max stands up.

MIMI

Oh, honey, don't go yet. We don't mind that you smell bad, shower later.

MAX

No . . . my feelings are hurt.

Everyone looks worried.

It'll do me good to freshen up.

SAFRON

Can we play a game before bedtime?

MAX

Anything you want, angel.

CUT TO:

INT. BATHROOM. EVENING

Max strips off. He looks in the mirror and sees with horror that the ink stain is still there. It looks like a huge birthmark over his heart.

CUT TO:

INT. SHOWER. EVENING

Max scrubs himself with a brush, his hair a mass of suds. He rinses off but the mark is still there, fainter, more like a big bruise. He scrubs again, harder this time.

CUT TO:

EXT. HOUSE. DUSK

Max plays a game with the kids. Very tactile and affectionate. They cling on to his legs and he tries to walk with them holding on. Mimi comes out.

MIMI

OK, monsters, bedtime.

KIDS

Five more minutes . . . five more minutes.

MIMI

You already had ten more minutes. Mummy and Daddy want to play now.

BRANFORD

What're you going to play, Dad?

SAFRON

Doctors and nurses.

MIMI

Bed . . . right now.

CUT TO:

INT. HOUSE. NIGHT

Max is sitting on the couch watching the news. Mimi comes in and straddles him, blocking the TV, her breasts in his face. Max nuzzles them. Oscar, the dog, follows her in and again begins sniffing Max. Max tries to shove the dog away without Mimi noticing but Oscar starts growling and then barks at Max. Mimi looks at Oscar and then at Max.

MIMI

Maybe she can smell another bitch on you. Is that possible?

Max breaks out in a sweat again, leans back on the couch. Mimi strokes his face and looks into his eyes. Looks at Oscar and then crouches down next to her, talks to her as if she was human.

What is it, Oscar? What is it? What are you trying to tell Momma? What? What?

Angle – on Max, going through agony, sweating. Comes to a decision.

MAX

OK . . . I'll tell you. You're going to hate me though.

Mimi and Oscar look at him. Max takes a deep breath, swallows hard.

When I was in New York . . . I . . . missed my flight . . . and I . . .

MIMI

I know what you're going to tell me. Oscar's not stupid, Max.

MAX

I know . . . I know.

MIMI

How many?

MAX

What?

MIMI

Did you smoke a whole pack, or was it just a few?

Max stares at her for a long time. We hear a snatch from the Grosse Fuge.

MAX

Just one, Mimi. Just one.

MIMI

Well, the smoke police are gonna have to watch you day and night, Mr Sinner. Now come to bed. I have a surprise for you, even though you don't deserve it.

CUT TO:

INT. BEDROOM. NIGHT

Max is in bed waiting for Mimi. The lights are on and it's pretty bright. He is reading a Balzac novel. The door from the bathroom opens and we hear Mimi quietly humming the theme from The Stripper. *A long leg makes an appearance, followed by the rest of Mimi. She is wearing some kind of black lingerie-cum-bedroom outfit. She clicks off the bedroom light but leaves on the bathroom light so that she is now back-lit. Max manages to put the book down just as she gets to the bed.*

MIMI

Do you like your surprise?

MAX

(forced enthusiasm)

Wow . . . it's great. Where did you get it?

MIMI

Victoria's Secret. I knew you'd like it . . . and I kept dropping hints . . . which you ignored, so I thought I'd get it myself.

(puts her hand under the sheets)

Do you think it's sexy?

MAX

Really sexy.

MIMI

(playing with him under the sheets)

How sexy?

Max plays with her breasts absent-mindedly. We see that they've probably had some surgery in that they defy gravity.

MAX

Incredibly sexy.

Mimi pulls back the sheet and looks down at Max's groin.

MIMI

You must be really tired, honey. You probably didn't get much sleep last night.

MAX

I'm not tired. Come here.

And he pulls her on to the bed . . .

FADE TO BLACK.

FADE UP TO:

INT. BEDROOM (LATER). NIGHT

In complete silence we see them making love. She is kneeling and Max is behind. It is hard work. Sweat is pouring off Max's face.

CUT TO:

Mimi having a very noisy (fake?) orgasm as Max pounds away from above her.

Camera shifts from his POV of her to her POV of him. The noise level increases as the real orgasm takes over from the fake.

CUT TO:

FLASH IMAGE: INT. RECITAL ROOMS. NIGHT

. . . of Karen as she turns to look at him at the concert.

BACK TO . . . :

INT. BEDROOM. NIGHT

Both of them about to come.

MIMI

Harder, Max. Harder. Ohhhhh.

He puts his hand over her mouth.

MAX

You'll frighten the kids.

MIMI

Fuck the kids, Max . . .

. . . and she makes more noise. Max balls up her panties and puts them in her mouth. Sweat drips off his face on to her face . . .

HARD CUT TO:

Max rolling off her and on to his back. Now they are both looking up to the camera. Breathing fast and shallow and exhausted. Max has his hands protectively placed over his groin. Mimi likewise. They both look exhausted.

MIMI

Was it good for you?

MAX

(flatly)

Fantastic. How about you?

MIMI
(*flatly*)

The best.

Max closes his eyes and starts to doze. Mimi is still pretty wired. She reaches for him and accidentally whacks him on the cheek. Max jumps awake, panicked for a split second.

MAX

What? What?

MIMI

I bought a video.

MAX

What kind of video?

MIMI

Guide to lovemaking. I think we should try some new stuff.

Camera moves in tight on Max's face. So . . . it wasn't *good for her.*

MAX

OK . . .

Mimi sits up and begins energetically rubbing his chest as if he needed heart massage.

MIMI

You want to watch some now?

MAX

Tomorrow.

Mimi squeezes his nipples and Max winces with pain. Mimi stares at his chest.

MIMI

Jesus, what did you do last night?

Max opens his eyes suddenly, looks at Mimi, then looks down at his chest.

MAX

Ink. I spilled ink . . .

FADE OUT.

In the black we hear a voice . . .

VOICE

Smoking will kill you. Smoking will kill the people you love. Smoking will kill you. Smoking will kill the people you love. Repeat after me.

VOICE PLUS MAX

Smoking will kill you. Smoking will kill the people you love. Smoking will kill you. Smoking will kill the people you love. Repeat after me . . .

FADE UP TO:

INT. MAX'S CAR. SAN VINCENTE BOULEVARD, SANTA MONICA. DAY

Max in a Porsche Carrera 4, bright red. Traffic is typical LA, moving but at a snail's pace.

VOICE PLUS MAX

Smoking will kill you . . . Smoking will kill the ones you love . . .

All around him people are doing things in their cars. Everyone is on a mobile phone. Most have coffee, some have food. Women are doing their make-up. Many are reading a newspaper or a book. On the green centre of the road a line of joggers wearing face masks and headphones pounds to and fro.

CUT TO:

INT. MAX'S OFFICE, THE AD AGENCY, RECEPTION AREA. DAY

Max walks briskly through and smiles at the Asian receptionist, who conducts two conversations at the same time with no discernible change of expression as she speaks into her designer headset. An entire wall is taken up with TV monitors displaying commercials that the company has made. In the waiting area a number of stunning but vacuous model types sit and leaf through magazines. When they see Max some of them smile.

RECEPTIONIST

I'm going to put you on hold for a moment . . . Good

morning, Mr West . . . JMD Advertising, how may I help you? One moment please . . .

MAX

Good morning, Amy. Did they start yet?

RECEPTIONIST

JMD Advertising, will you hold please? . . . I just took them coffee. They're waiting for you . . . Thank you for holding. How may I connect you? Did you have fun in New York? You bad boy . . .

Max turns around and sees that she is talking to someone on the phone.

CUT TO:

INT. ENTRANCE TO CONFERENCE ROOM. DAY

Max hesitates by the door, listens to the voices inside. Conversations about marketing strategy, surveys, whatever. After a long pause, Max goes in.

CUT TO:

INT. CONFERENCE ROOM. DAY

Don is at the head of the table, he's the boss. George is there also. The other players are Malinda, a heavy-set woman in her forties, Nathan, who's in his thirties, and Margaux. Mickey is also there and immediately gets up and kisses him. She has got him a cappuccino. Although this is essentially a comic scene, the playing of it is deadly serious. On the table is a selection of huge jars of pickles and gherkins.

DON

Hey . . . look who made it back.

GEORGE

Looking none the worse for wear . . .

MARGAUX

Hi, Max.

MAX

Hi, Margaux. Morning, everyone. Sorry I'm late. Traffic was bad.

NATHAN

Yeah, we noticed. Can we start soon? I have another meeting at ten-thirty.

DON

(*to Max*)

You're ready for this?

MAX

Sure.

DON

It's boring but lucrative. They've seen your show reel and they like it. Just take them through some ideas. I think it best if we keep it fairly conservative for now.

HARD CUT TO:

INT. CONFERENCE ROOM (FIFTEEN MINUTES LATER). DAY

Same people plus some suits. Phil Hill and his sidekick, Merv. Two very straight-looking men. Although this is not a conventional pitch meeting, it's more a mixture of different meetings, there is good comic possibility. Margaux needs to smoke all the time so would place herself at an open window. Mickey thinks that anything Max does is genius. George gets over-excited and doesn't know quite where the lines are. Don is dull and macho and sees himself as Burt Lancaster or similar. The two suits are rich but from way out of town and Max has no patience with this and is in a world of his own imagination which has a lot to do with Karen.

PHIL HILL

Hi, my name's Phil Hill but in fact I'm known as 'Phil the Dill'. I am the President of the International Pickle Association . . .

DON

(*sounding impressed*)

International?

PHIL HILL

(*chuckling*)

Well, actually it is national, but with the help of this campaign

I see no reason why we couldn't expand a little. Merv?

The other suit speaks.

MERV

The Pickle Association doesn't just limit itself to pickle workers . . .

PHIL HILL

No, sir.

MERV

You see . . .

(*dramatic*)

. . . pickles are seasonal.

Mickey is having a very hard time keeping a straight face and Max does nothing to help her. As the meeting progresses she gets the giggles in a bad way and will have to resort to stuff like nose-blowing and pinching herself.

PHIL HILL

And so is sauerkraut.

MERV

So we're talking about an association that represents the rights of the pickle and sauerkraut workers of the entire west coast of America.

Phil the Dill reaches out for one of the huge jars of dills and unscrews the lid. He takes a dill and then slides the jar towards Don.

PHIL HILL

Let's start off on the right foot here.

Don takes one and slides the jar to the next person. Eventually everyone except Max will have sampled the dills. They are huge and phallic and again humour is never too far away.

MALINDA

George and Margaux already did some research and came up with some interesting stuff. Why don't you start, Margaux?

MARGAUX

Thanks, guys. So . . . what we're thinking about is this, and it's just an idea, nothing written in stone . . .

Max is drawing something on his pad as he listens, a curving line. Watched by Mickey.

GEORGE

. . . We could try and do a hot dog association campaign.

DON

Interesting.

PHIL HILL

Exciting.

MARGAUX

(*gathering momentum*)

I think so. We wed sauerkraut to the dog. We find the foremost hot dog expert in the country, some German from Minnesota, someone whose family have been making hot dogs for generations . . .

GEORGE

. . . we get him to talk about how good, how traditional it is to have sauerkraut with the dog. To put it in a nutshell, we piggyback on the dog . . .

MARGAUX

. . . everyone loves a dog.

MERV

(*explaining*)

Yes . . . this is a very bad time for sauerkraut. It's not exactly designer food and we really have to target the under-twenty-ones. Now . . . the thing we have to be very careful about is the balance between sauerkraut and the pickle.

Murmurs of agreement. Good point, Merv.

Angle – Max . . . is still drawing. We see that it is a breast not unlike Karen's breast. Mickey sees what it is and smiles at Max, like, what a great artist you are, Max.

PHIL HILL

Let's say you do a successful campaign, you do piggyback the dog and sell the sauerkraut, it cannot be at the expense of the pickle.

Margaux scribbles a note and passes it to Don.

DON

Nathan?

NATHAN

Couple of ideas, in no particular order of importance . . .

Max starts work on the rest of the body in the drawing. Don is watching him curiously.

. . . pickle Christmas tree decorations that we can send out to the food editors . . .

FLASHBACK – *maybe superimposed on top of existing scene:*

INT. HOTEL BEDROOM. DAWN

Max is dressed and ready to go. Karen is sitting up in bed smoking a cigarette. Lots of pillows supporting her, naked except for the sheet. Max comes to sit on the bed.

KAREN

No names, no telephone numbers, OK?

MAX

Yeah.

But he doesn't want to leave. He takes the cigarette from her and drags deeply, then stubs it out. He pulls the sheet down and reveals her breast. She holds it for him.

KAREN

We're not going to lie to each other. This never happened and we're never going to see each other again . . .

MAX

It's OK. You don't have to say it.

BACK TO:

INT. CONFERENCE ROOM. DAY

NATHAN

You know that weather guy who wears a different costume for each show? We send him a pickle suit. Then we send him a sauerkraut and hot dog suit. Two suits . . . two shows.

Phil the Dill is nodding but he's not won over yet. He's nervous.

DON

Now we're cooking. What do you think, Max?

(*to Phil the Dill*)

Max is the guy who would be making the films, the commercial spots. You saw his reel.

PHIL HILL

Aha!

MAX

Yeah, good things, good ideas.

DON

Do you have ideas? I see you sketching there.

Max holds up the drawing for all to see. It's quite an explicit nude now. He puts the drawing down and thinks for a moment. They are all waiting for him.

MAX

How about this? A series of spots. Funny but serious. We set up a National Pickle Award. *The* National Pickle Award . . .

MICKEY

That's such a great idea.

MARGAUX

Who gets it?

MAX

Anyone famous who's in a pickle. We send him or her a huge plastic pickle and be there as they open the door, film the whole thing on Dig or Hi-8, Video Diary style. Get the girl who did the MTV news to do it for us . . .

They stare at Max, not quite sure if he's having them on or not. Max throws caution to the winds.

We make a list of . . . a list people, starting with the president . . . Michael Jackson . . . O.J. . . . whoever. We keep our noise to the *National Enquirer* and find out who is going to be in a pickle and then . . . WHAM . . . What do you think, Phil, Mr Hill . . . Merv?

Silence. Everyone staring.

He was buried in his hot dog and sauerkraut bun. It was no big dill. We really relished him. That kind of thing.

PHIL HILL

What is that?

MAX

My epitaph! I'd like that as my epitaph.

CUT TO:

INT. CORRIDOR. DAY

Don and Margaux catch up with Max, who is walking with Mickey, who is doubled and almost sick with letting out her laughter at last.

DON

Not so funny, Max.

MAX

No? I think it could work. It's a little offbeat perhaps, but . . .

MARGAUX

I think everyone thought you were just being snotty. Max, the genius, makes fun of the little people.

MAX

No, not at all, Margaux. Not at all. I was serious. If you . . . we . . . want to give the pickle a high profile then we have to come up with something pretty outrageous. No half measures. Speaking personally I'd rather be dead than have that shit on my show reel. Come on, Don. Let's stop and think about the profile of the company for a moment, shall we? Did we start this hip little show to have the Green Pean on the screen? I don't think so. If it's just about numbers I'm out of here, OK!

They stop by the coffee machine and fill cups. Don sees that Max's anger is real and calms down. Max is more valuable than Phil the Dill.

CUT TO:

EXT. SAN VICENTE BOULEVARD. EVENING

Same crawling traffic, this time going in the opposite direction. Max is again listening to his anti-smoking tape. The traffic grinds to a halt. Meanwhile the traffic in the opposite direction is flowing quickly. Max changes tapes. It is a Beethoven string quartet.

Wide shot of freeway – music fills the soundtrack.

MAX

(*voice-over*)

The next year was a tough one. Everything in my life seemed to be changing at the same time and there was nothing I could do except watch.

MONTAGE:

INT. THEATRE. DAY

Max making a commercial. Lots of glamour and models and perfume and clothes . . .

MAX

(*voice-over*)

It was as if I didn't exist. I could see myself and I could hear myself but I was detached from the whole process. I loved my wife, I adored my kids but . . . I wasn't me any more.

FADE TO BLACK.

TITLE: SIX MONTHS LATER

CUT TO:

INT. MAX'S HOUSE. NIGHT

Close-up on a TV screen. A beautifully made commercial, as good as it gets, not glossy, just good . . . hip . . . whatever . . .

Camera pulls back to reveal . . .

. . . a dinner party. All of the guys from work and their wives are there, as well as some friends of Mimi's. Mimi looks fantastic in a very sexy black dress which is extremely short and low-cut. The kids are still up. Mimi tells them they have to go to bed now. Everyone congratulates Max as if he'd just directed a Bergman film. Don opens a bottle of champagne and they all toast Max.

Other guests include Don, his wife, Marie, who is a nervy bleached blonde who drinks too much at parties like this one. Everyone from the business is there.

DON

To the smartass . . . who was right again.

DISSOLVE TO:

INT. MAX'S HOUSE (LATER). NIGHT

Everyone eating pasta and talking about Aids. Don is making the point that, tragic though the disease is, homosexuality is not a natural thing and there has to be a payoff somewhere down the line. Someone makes a joke about gays and everyone (except Max) laughs. Mimi comes in with the coffee.

MIMI

What'd I miss, you guys?

And she leans across the table to put the milk jug down. Her dress is low-cut she doesn't need a bra. Don gazes at her breasts and Max takes note.

DON

I was just saying I don't get the gay thing . . . I mean . . . I know we all supposed to be so goddamn liberal and all but . . .

And he raises his hands as if he were cupping two large breasts

. . . women are natural . . . men are not.

MAX

You ever kiss a man, Don?

DON

No thank you, sir. You?

MAX

Sure.

DISSOLVE TO:

INT. MAX'S HOUSE (LATER STILL). NIGHT

Sitting around on sofas and chairs.

DON

I thought it was pretty incredible. There we were in the middle of the jungle, for Chrissakes, in the middle of the Third World . . .

(*looks around for full attention*)

. . . and we could go to our room and turn on the TV and get CNN and find out exactly what was happening in the world.

MIMI

It is pretty incredible when you think about it. I would always ask before booking a holiday in a place like that if they . . . you know . . . if they had CNN.

Nathan's wife, Malissa, is American Asian.

MALISSA

Most of them do now. We stayed in a lot . . . And MTV.

DON

Boy, some of that stuff is pretty hard-core. I'm surprised they get away with it . . . particularly some of the new black stuff.

GEORGE

(*English accent*)

Ghastly music.

Mickey is there, sitting next to Max, bored by all of this.

MAX

Ah . . . MTV.

Mickey laughs as if this were pretty funny and looks into Max's eyes as she lights a small joint.

MARIE

Don won't leave the country because of the water.

MIMI

What's with the water, Don?

DON

We have no control over the water in the rest of the world. We have no idea what is in it. So you get some infection in the middle of nowhere and then have to risk some doctor with a qualification from . . . Bogotá University.

Mickey passes the joint to Max, who inhales deeply. Mimi watches disapprovingly.

MALISSA

Right. Don has a good point there.

MAX

So drink bottled water.

Max offers the joint to Don.

DON

No thanks. They proved that bottled water is as dangerous as tap water.

Max takes another deep drag and offers it to Mimi, who makes a quick face of disapproval and says no. Marie is interested, however, and joins Max on the couch.

MAX

Who proved?

MALISSA

I saw it on some TV thing.

MAX

TV is the worst fucking thing that ever happened to this country . . .

Things get a little quieter. Marie, now on the sofa with Max and Mickey, hands the joint back to Max, who drags deep again.

MALISSA

I don't think so . . . What do you mean?

MAX

I mean . . . we all watch TV talk shows, TV news, whatever . . . everything is reduced to thirty-second soundbites with cute human-interest stories to cushion the facts. TV isn't the news, TV isn't the world, it's shit, it's absolute crap.

DON

(*laughing*)

Look out . . . Max's turning into a commie fag. Kissing guys and smoking dope. Hey, hello, the sixties are over, Max.

MAX

Fuck you, Don.

Now things are really quiet.

MIMI

How about some ice cream. We have Baileys Haagen-Dazs.

Exaggerated sounds of childish enthusiasm from everyone as Mimi heads for the kitchen. Max holds up the last of the joint.

MAX

You sure you don't want some? It's very good.

MARIE

Yes, please.

CUT TO:

EXT./INT. HOUSE (LATER). NIGHT

Max and Mimi clearing up. She is in a bad mood.

MIMI

Well . . . that finished the party off.

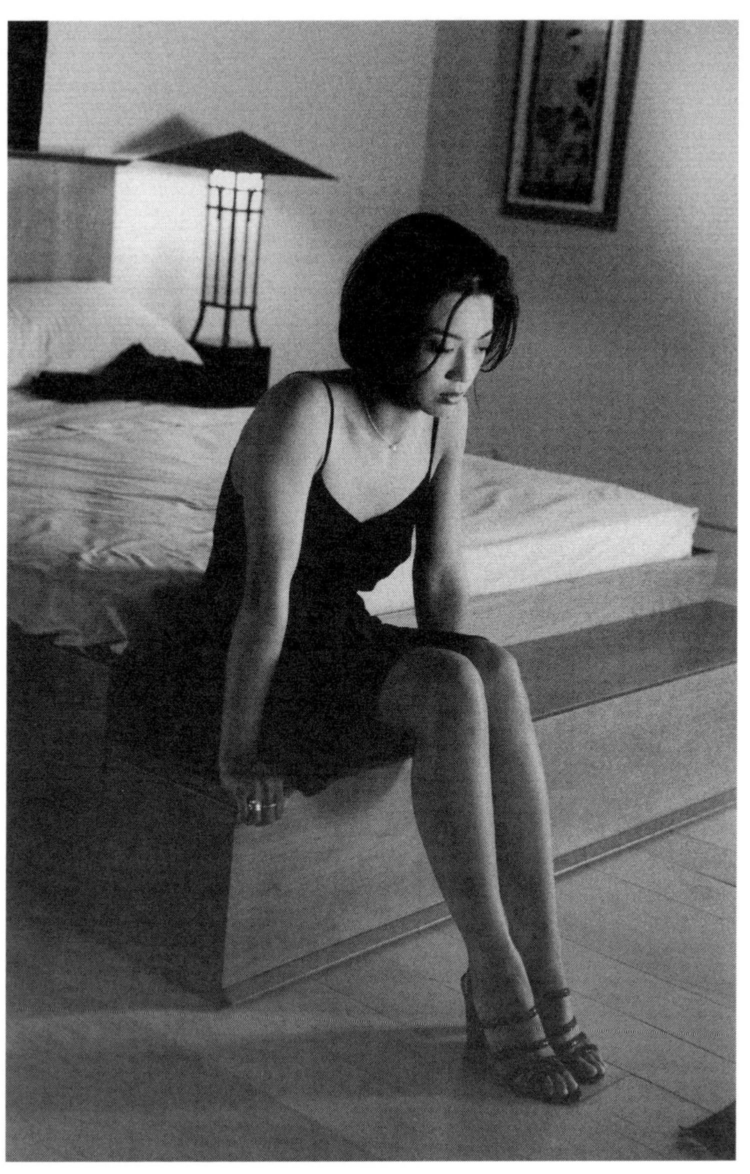

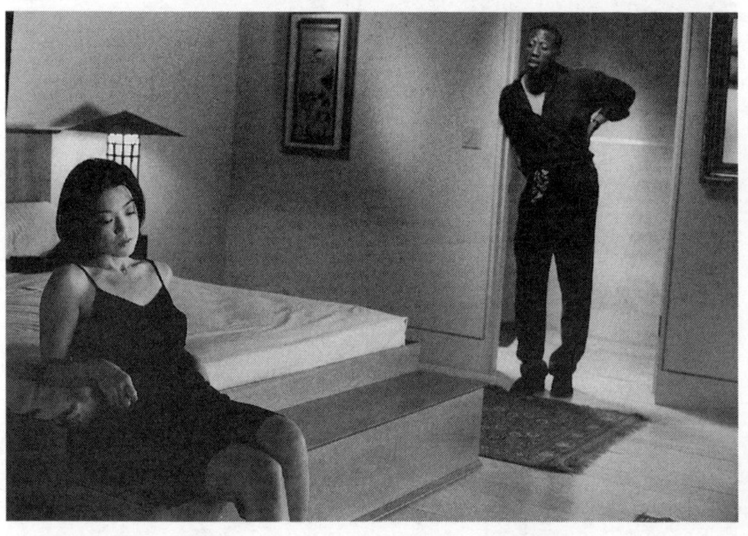

MAX

Sorry. I thought it might open it up a bit. I thought we could have a real conversation for a change.

MIMI

I don't think so.

MAX

You don't think so?

MIMI

Everyone was having a good time and then you decided to make it serious. It's like you have to let everyone know what a deep thinker you are and how stupid we all are.

MAX

I don't think that's true. Not everyone . . . is . . .

MIMI

. . . stupid? Your assistant, for example.

MAX

Mickey? Oh, come on.

Mimi stops and looks at him, puts her head to one side.

MIMI

She hangs on every word you say. Are you fucking her?

Max looks puzzled.

MAX

Why do you say that?

MIMI

Someone has to be getting it, and it sure as hell ain't me. She'd like you to fuck her.

Mimi stops what she is doing for a moment and looks at him.

MAX

(*puzzled*)

Really?

MIMI

Really. Or how about Marie? She seemed to find you fascinating suddenly.

Mimi opens the dishwasher and begins loading.

MAX

Maybe the reason she suddenly found me fascinating . . .

MIMI

. . . and wants you to fuck her . . .

MAX

. . . and would like me to make love to her . . . is because her husband spent most of the evening looking down the front of your new dress.

Mimi finishes the loading and stands up straight.

MIMI

So you don't like it?

MAX

The dress is fine. It depends on how you wear it.

Mimi goes red as her temper gets out of control.

MIMI

Well, I think you may be in the minority there. And to be honest, it's nice to know that some men still find me attractive.

MAX

You're attractive . . . OK! You don't need to expose your breasts to be constantly endorsed.

MIMI

(*shouting*)

I was not . . . Fuck you.

MAX

Do you know that when you lean forward like that you can see your nipples?

MIMI

Fuck you.

MAX

I mean . . . when you buy a dress or a blouse that's low-cut . . . do you practise with it in front of a mirror? Do you work it all out . . . a lean this far exposes so much breast . . . a lean this far exposes just the pink area around the nipple . . . but a lean this far gives everything for just a second? Or do you forget all about it?

MIMI

You must be really stoned. What the fuck are you talking about?

Max walks towards her.

MAX

Come on, let's test the theory.

And Max takes her by the arm and walks her to a mirror.

Give it a lean . . . Go on . . .

He tries to make her bend forward. She resists and then gives him a backhander across the face. He raises his hand and then stops it in mid-strike. They look at each other.

CUT TO:

INT. MAX'S HOUSE (LATER). EARLY MORNING

Max is trying to sleep on the sofa with a blanket over him. Safron comes in and looks at him curiously, then gets into bed with him. Moments later Branford comes in with a teddy bear and gets in also. Max has an arm around each of them.

SAFRON

Daddy . . . are you and Mom getting a divorce?

MAX

Don't be silly. We just had a fight, that's all.

BRANFORD

Who won?

MAX

The winner always gets the bed.

SAFRON

I think the sofa's better than a bed.

MAX

Yeah, it's pretty good, isn't it?

BRANFORD

Can we watch some TV?

MAX

Ummmm . . . OK. But we have to keep the noise right down.

SAFRON

I'll get some food, shall I?

CUT TO:

INT. MAX'S HOUSE (LATER). MORNING

Safron is asleep on Max's chest. Branford and Max are watching a cartoon. Coke cans are in evidence.

CUT TO:

INT. DINING AREA. THE NEXT EVENING

Family mealtime. The food is eaten in silence. The kids are aware of the deal and watch both parents carefully. The atmosphere is intensely cool. We hear a car pull up outside and a horn is honked.

SAFRON

Can we go now?

MAX

Where?

BRANFORD

We're staying over at Nathan's. Mom said it was OK.

Mimi goes with them to the door.

MIMI

I've packed a bag for you, it's by the door. I'll pick you up tomorrow morning.

KIDS

(*as they leave*)

Bye, Mom. Bye, Dad.

There is a void left behind once they are gone.

INT. MAX'S HOUSE (LATER). NIGHT

Max pours himself a large Scotch. Mimi comes into the room wearing pink lycra and carrying a canvas bag.

MIMI

I'm going to work out. I'll see you later.

CUT TO:

INT. BEDROOM (LATER). NIGHT

Max lies on the bed and then wriggles uncomfortably. He fishes in the bedding and comes up with a video tape. He tosses it across the room.

INT. BEDROOM (LATER). NIGHT

Max is on the bed reading another Balzac novel. We hear bathroom noises. Bottles being moved, teeth being brushed. Max's face is a blank. Mimi comes into the room wearing a white T-shirt and black panties.

MAX

How was the gym?

MIMI

Fantastic. I feel great.

He looks at her as she goes to the vanity unit and brushes her gorgeous hair. Max is pretty stoned.

Max . . . I think you should spank me.

MAX

What for?

MIMI

Because I'd like you to.

MAX

(*to himself*)

Ah . . . the video.

She walks over to the bed. Max sits up as she kneels on the bed over him.

MIMI

It's perfectly normal and healthy, Max. Everyone does it.

She lies flat over his thighs.

MAX

They do? Who, for example?

Max looks down at her perfect body, her perfectly shaped bottom, covered in black rayon.

MIMI

Marie and Don.

MAX

How do you know?

MIMI

She came with me to buy the dress.

Max slides her T-shirt up a little and strokes her bottom in a friendly way.

MAX

What else did you talk about?

MIMI

You . . . That's how I know she wants to fuck you. She suggested a foursome.

MAX

And what did you say?

Max spanks her lightly.

MIMI

I said I would talk to the man of the house about it . . . Harder . . . you can do it harder . . . if you want to.

MAX

What was she suggesting, all of us together . . . or me and Marie . . . you and Don?

MIMI

Would you like me to fuck Nathan?

Max spanks her quite hard.

Ow.

MAX

Sorry . . . Was that too hard?

MIMI

No . . . it's OK. Do it again.

MAX

Where? Here . . . or here?

MIMI

Yes . . . there.

Max strokes her for a while and then raises his hand, hesitates . . . Camera goes in tight on his face. He seems lost.

Max . . . do you want to fuck Marie?

He spanks her harder.

CUT TO:

FLASHBACK: INT. HOTEL BEDROOM. NIGHT

Flash image of Karen.

CUT TO:

INT. BEDROOM (LATER). NIGHT

The last seconds of a huge orgasm from Mimi as she pins Max to the bed and fucks him from above.

MIMI

Yes . . . fuck me . . . Oh yes, Max, Max, give me an O . . . Give me an R . . . give me a G . . . give me an A . . . gimme an ESSSSS . . . give . . . me . . . an – Oh my God, Max, yes, yes, yes . . .

She collapses on him and her huge hair covers his face and he has to push it away to breathe.

CUT TO:

INT. BEDROOM (LATER). NIGHT

The two of them lying together about to go to sleep.

MAX

Is it true what you said about Marie?

She puts her tongue in his ear and whispers . . .

MIMI

No. I just wanted to get you hard. Goodnight.

And she rolls over and goes to sleep.

FADE TO BLACK.

TITLE: SIX MONTHS LATER

CUT TO:

INT. BEDROOM. MORNING

Max wakes to the gentle sound of Mimi snoring. Her hair is different, blonder, shorter, longer . . . something. Max is the same, a little darker under the eyes perhaps. He eases himself out of bed without waking her.

EXT. MAX'S HOUSE. DAY

A beautiful California day. The Postman walks up to the front door and leaves a letter. We see Max (through the glass) come and pick it up, open it and read.

MAX

(*voice-over*)

The letter from Charlie should not have been a shock . . . but it was. He was in the hospital and didn't expect to come out. I'd called him a couple of times and he'd been joking and

OK. I'd promised to come over and see him but somehow that had never happened . . . It'd been a busy year . . . the usual excuses . . .

CUT TO:

EXT. NEW YORK STREETS. EARLY MORNING

Max gets out of a yellow cab with a small suitcase. He pays the fare and turns to look at . . .

Angle – hospital building.

MAX

(*voice-over*)

. . . but I realized the time for excuses had passed. But still I dreaded what I was going to see when I walked into Charlie's room.

CUT TO:

INT. HOSPITAL CORRIDORS. EARLY MORNING

Max walks through various areas. We get the sense of fear of hospitals. Everything is unfamiliar. A Priest and two Nuns come out of a room and Max shudders. Max peeks into the room and a very thin man is in bed. He and Max look at each other with no recognition. A Nurse comes in and asks Max who he is looking for.

CUT TO:

INT. CHARLIE'S HOSPITAL ROOM. EARLY MORNING

Charlie is very thin, sitting up in bed propped up by lots of pillows. He is on a drip and has a plastic oxygen mask over his mouth and nose. The oxygen mask gives off a hissing noise. A radio is playing classical music quietly. Max waves hello to Charlie, who makes a weak move with his hand on the bed and raises his eyebrows. There is another man in the room. About the same age as Max. He is wearing smart clothes. He and Max nod at each other and Max realizes that he knows him but is not sure where from. A Nurse comes in.

NURSE

If I could ask you guys to step outside for a moment while we give Charles his bath.

The two men do as they are told.

CUT TO:

INT. CORRIDOR. EARLY MORNING

The other man offers his hand to Max, who notices that he is wearing a surgical glove. They shake.

OTHER MAN

Good to see you, Max. My God, it must be fifteen years.

Max's expression gives him away.

It's Vernon, Charlie's brother.

MAX

Vernon, of course, great to see you. Forgive me. How are you?

VERNON

Just great, Max.

(*lowering his voice*)

Sorry we had to meet in such tragic circumstances, but I hear things are going great for you . . .

Over Vernon's shoulder Max can see the nurses moving Charlie in his bed. He is weak and delicate. On the soundtrack we hear some sad Beethoven and Vernon's voice fades down.

MAX

(*voice-over*)

Now I remembered Vernon – a real bore, the straight member of the family. He had everything arranged at the hospital, he'd appointed himself director. He told me that the doctors thought Charlie wouldn't make it past the next seven days. I mean, he wasn't a bad guy and he was certainly helping Charlie, but . . . I was glad when he left and I could talk to Charlie myself. Also I was in shock. I wouldn't have recognized Charlie if his name hadn't been on the door.

CUT TO:

INT. CHARLIE'S HOSPITAL ROOM. EARLY MORNING

Max sits next to the bed. Charlie is asleep and Max studies his face. Charlie opens his eyes and sees Max, smiles.

CHARLIE

How ya doin', buddy?

MAX

Pretty good. How about you?

CHARLIE

Mmmmm . . . so-so. Pretty tired as a matter of fact, can't sleep. You come by yourself?

MAX

Sure. Mimi's coming over later.

CHARLIE

Hey, I must be pretty sick if Mimi's coming.

(*laughs*)

You didn't recognize Vern. Vuuuuurn. Still the same prick but he's family so I love him, of course.

Max is glad to be on a neutral topic.

MAX

What's he do now?

CHARLIE

He lives upstate, near Albany, making a pile of dough in real estate.

MAX

Married?

CHARLIE

Yeah . . . very nice lady. I get on with her better than him. No kids yet because Vern wants to wait, what for I don't know, but he's waiting for something. Thanks for coming. It's good to see you.

MAX

It's great to see you.

CHARLIE

How long can you stay?

Max holds up his hands and smiles.

That long. You don't have to.

They fall silent and Max helps himself to an orange, offers some to Charlie, who declines.

I have these fucking sores on the inside of my mouth . . . what a mess. Listen, I'm sure Vern told you the score . . . It's better for me if we can be open about the thing . . . OK?

MAX

Sure. He told me. I want to be useful, Charlie. Just tell me what you want and I'll do it.

CHARLIE

Right . . . starting now I'd like you to try and get me in a more comfortable position.

Max comes to the bed and sits Charlie up. He fluffs the pillows and gets him comfortable, then sits on the bed next to him and holds his hand.

MAX

What else?

CHARLIE

I'd like some really good grass.

MAX

OK. Next!

CHARLIE

I'd like to ease off on the visits. Everyone is coming and it's very tiring, which means that the people I want to see don't get me at my best. I know you can deal with it without upsetting or offending anyone. Vern is a bit too official, you know.

MAX

Sure, I can do that. You just tell me what you want. Next!

CHARLIE

That's it for now.

MAX

What's the best time for me to visit?

CHARLIE

Graveyard shift. My lover comes in the evening but he has to go back to his family at night.

Max nods but doesn't probe this complication.

Dawn is the worst time for me. I get very scared. I shit my pants with fear of death. I'd appreciate you being around.

MAX

Hey . . . I'll be there, buddy.

CUT TO:

INT. HOTEL. DAY

Max checks back into hotel. Is welcomed by the same desk clerk.

EXT. NEW YORK STREETS. PRE-DAWN

Max walking the deserted streets on his way to the hospital. Some mellow music.

MAX

(*voice-over*)

So that's what I did for the next week. Charlie had no intention of keeping to Vern's schedule but nearly every morning I felt that I was watching a man about to die . . .

INT. CHARLIE'S HOSPITAL ROOM. DAWN

In the near-dark we see Charlie struggling for breath with his oxygen mask over his mouth. Max watching him, his face tight, knowing there is nothing he can really do except be there.

MAX

(*voice-over*)

. . . but then he'd pull it all together and make it through the morning. The people who looked after him were saints . . .

Charlie being comforted by doctors and nurses. There is something saint-like about them as they deal with all problems and still have enough compassion left for the soul of the patient.

. . . and every time I said bye to Charlie I thought it might be the last time . . .

Max leaving the room in a businesslike way.

OK, baby, I'm outta here. Need anything from the store, some decent food?

CHARLIE

Sure, pastrami on rye, hold the mustard.

MAX

You got it, pal. How about some of that papaya juice? You liked it the other day. It's very mild. It won't hurt your mouth.

CHARLIE

All right . . . thanks, man.

Max is almost out of the door . . .

Max!

Max stops.

I'm really glad you're here. What you're doing is great, but . . .

MAX

What?

CHARLIE

I worry about you. You're not happy. I want you to be happy, you know. You're my friend, Max.

Max comes closer to the bed.

MAX

I'm all right. Really.

CHARLIE

Sure. But don't forget . . . life is short, man. Remember what they used to say, those hippies . . . this isn't a rehearsal, it's the real thing.

MAX

(*laughing*)

Fuck you, Charlie. See you at seven, right?

CHARLIE

I'm not going anywhere.

CUT TO:

EXT. BUSY NEW YORK STREETS. 10 A.M.

Max walking away from the hospital. He stops to light a cigarette. He needs a shave. His eyes are wet.

He walks some more.

CUT TO:

INT. SUBWAY STATION. DAY

Max waiting for a train. He looks at a poster for the Quartetto Italiano.

MAX
(*voice-over*)

I realized that he was going to die. Of course I'd known that all along, but up until that moment it was an abstract idea and now it was a reality. What it meant was that Charlie was going to leave soon and he wouldn't be coming back. Death is so fucking strange. Everything in me that was hollow and false seemed so clear suddenly. And everything looked stunning and beautiful. The people in the street, the buildings. I rang the hospital on an impulse . . .

CUT TO:

EXT. A PAYPHONE SOMEWHERE IN THE CITY. DAY

MAX
(*voice-over*)

. . . and asked them if it would be possible to rent a limo and take him for a drive, get him into the sunlight. But they said it would kill him and . . . well, there's not a lot to say to that. Well, I must have walked ten miles that day. New York is the most beautiful city in the world. And I got back to the hospital a little late. Charlies was sure fooling a lot of people . . .

CUT TO:

INT. CHARLIE'S HOSPITAL ROOM. NIGHT

The room is full of gay men and actors. Charlie is dressed up and very animated. The mood is very happy and funny. Charlie is telling a story about a show that went wrong and everyone is laughing. A joint is being passed around. Max observes, not really knowing the people. Charlie's lover, Peter, is sitting on the bed with him. Max sits by the door, happy for Charlie. The door opens and two more visitors come in. The first is Vernon, the second is masked by the door. Vernon is awkward with the gay men and the theatrical buzz.

VERNON

Hey, everyone, how's it all going?

The party continues. Vernon sees Max and takes a place next to him, glad to see a safe face.

Hey, Max, how's it going?

Max nods hello.

Like you to meet my wife . . .

And he ushers her in from the doorway.

Angle – Max. Max looks up and smiles. We hold the shot for as long as we can. Max stares at Vernon's wife.

Max's POV – it is Karen. She looks at Max. Only a little movement in her eyes gives anything away.

FADE TO BLACK.

FADE UP FROM BLACK – SCENE CONTINUES:

Max . . . Karen . . . Karen . . . Max.

Max stands and offers his hand. Karen takes it.

MAX

Nice to meet you.

KAREN

You too.

Karen stares at Max, her face shows no expression. She goes over to the bed and kisses Charlie warmly. Vernon looks like he doesn't really approve of this, as in, 'We know it's supposed to be safe, but can we really be sure?' Charlie is really pleased to see Karen and it is clear that they are very fond of each other.

Max and Vernon hang by the door.

VERNON

When's your wife coming in?

MAX

Um . . . tomorrow.

VERNON

Great, we should all have dinner. I know a great new place. You like sushi?

FADE TO BLACK.

FADE UP ON:

INT. MAX'S HOTEL ROOM. DAY

Max is asleep, the blinds are closed. The door opens and Mimi comes in with a suitcase. She yawns deeply as she undresses down to her underwear and gets into bed with Max and snuggles up to him. Max, still asleep, responds and puts his arm around her and she is asleep in a minute.

Angle – Max . . . as he wakes up and for a moment has no idea where he is or who he is with. It is dark in the room. He looks down at Mimi, who is sleeping on her back, one breast exposed. Max covers her and brushes the hair off her face. He looks at his watch.

CUT TO:

INT. HOSPITAL CORRIDOR. NIGHT

Max and Mimi (carrying a huge bunch of flowers) walk towards Charlie's room. She is visibly nervous. A pitifully thin man is walking with a stick, helped by a man and a woman (mother and father?). Max takes her arm as they arrive at the door.

Angle – Mimi's POV of Charlie. She is shocked by what she sees and moves out of Charlie's eyeline.

MAX

Listen . . . it's OK if you don't come in. He'll understand. There's a bar across the street. Wait for me there.

MIMI

No. I'll be fine. I just need a moment to . . .

Mimi is in tears and has to make a big effort to pull herself together. This is an important moment. We may have written her off in some ways but she does have a heart.

CUT TO:

INT. CHARLIE'S HOSPITAL ROOM. NIGHT

Max and Mimi come in. She has got her act together and is smiling and cheerful but strange. (It is interesting to play this from Charlie's POV. This must happen a lot to sick people; their friends start treating them like strangers.)

Mimi comes to the bed and mimes a kiss but doesn't actually touch him. Charlie asks her how she is and how the kids are and how old are the kids now and how long is it since we saw each other and then segues into another conversation with some of the actors, and in the background we see Vernon and Karen coming in and she has an identical bunch of flowers.

Suddenly all four of them, Karen, Mimi, Vernon and Max, are standing together near the bed.

CHARLIE

(*talking about flowers*)

These are lovely. I think there's some vases over by the sink.

KAREN

Thanks, sweetheart. How're ya feeling tonight?

Charlie raises his eyebrows as Karen comes over to give him a gentle hug. She sits him forward and fluffs his pillow. Vernon, as ever, looks worried by Karen's contact with him.

VERNON

Hi, kiddo. Listen . . . I can't come in for a few days, gotta go back and earn some money, but Max'll be here to mind the fort.

Charlie squeezes Vernon's gloved hand to say it's all right.

Mimi gives Max a 'Why don't you introduce everyone?' look.

MAX

Vernon, this is Mimi . . . my wife.

VERNON

Really nice to meet you, Mimi. Max told me you were coming in. I'm hoping we can all get together.

MAX

And this is . . .

KAREN

Hi . . . Karen. Nice to meet you, Mimi.

The two women check each other out. A group of Charlie's friends arrive, making a lot of cheerful noise. The room is now a little too full and clearly it's time to leave.

VERNON

Is anyone hungry?

Looks are exchanged and Mimi nods that she could eat something.

CUT TO:

INT. SUSHI RESTAURANT. NIGHT

Max and Mimi on one side of a table across from Vernon and Karen. A Japanese waitress brings a huge plate of food and serves them all. They eat in silence for a while. Max and Karen are sitting opposite each other. Vernon and Mimi do all of the talking.

MIMI

We bought it just after the earthquake and of course the riots and the floods and the mudslides . . .

VERNON

(*laughing*)

. . . very smart, very smart. Lowest house prices since before the gold rush. We were very tempted to move out at that time – well, I was . . . it was trickier for Karen, for her business.

MIMI

What do you do, Karen?

KAREN

I'm a rocket scientist.

There is a silence.

VERNON

Karen works for the Fairchild Group.

MIMI

Oh!

VERNON

They make small rockets for telephone systems, that kind of thing. Fairchild closed their West Coast division last year. That's why it was difficult to make the move.

Max stares at Karen. A rocket scientist? She glances at him and then concentrates on her food.

MIMI

Do you live in New York?

VERNON

Upstate. We have a house outside Albany. How long are you staying?

MIMI

Just a few days. I have to get back to the kids. This must be very difficult for you.

VERNON

Yes, it is. But . . . it's something we've been expecting, you know . . . The life these guys lead . . . I don't know . . .

Vernon chokes up a bit and drinks some saki and then turns to Max.

It's great that you could find time for this, Max. It means a lot to him.

MAX

It means a lot to me too, Vern. Anyway . . . here's to Charlie.

Max raises his saki and he and Vernon clink, then Mimi and Vernon . . . and then Max and Karen.

VERNON

We have to go home tomorrow. Look, here's my card. Call me if . . . I can be there in two hours.

CUT TO:

EXT. RESTAURANT. NIGHT

The couples say goodnight to each other.

INT. MAX'S HOTEL ROOM. NIGHT

Both moving around each other in the bathroom. Max cleaning his teeth. Mimi putting stuff on her face.

MIMI

How much longer do you have to stay?

MAX

As long as it takes.

MIMI

Well, how long is that?

MAX

Ask me in the morning and I'd say it was a matter of hours . . . but then in the evening he looks great again. Three weeks ago the doctors said two weeks.

MIMI

What about work?

MAX

What about it?

MIMI

I don't think they're very happy about you not being there.

MAX

Too bad. This is more important.

Mimi walks into the bedroom, out of hearing range.

MIMI

That's not a very smart thing to say. We have a mortgage and two kids.

MAX

(*to himself*)

Don't worry. He'll die soon.

CUT TO:

INT. MAX'S HOTEL ROOM (LATER). NIGHT

In bed with the lights off.

MIMI

Vernon seems like a very nice man.

MAX

Yeah, he is.

MIMI

What do you make of her?

MAX

Yeah . . . she seems nice.

MIMI

You think so?

MAX

Yeah, she seems OK. You didn't like her?

MIMI

Mmmm . . . not really. I couldn't see what he'd see in her. He's a good-looking guy and she's kind of ordinary, mousy. Don't you think?

MAX

Yeah . . . maybe. I've got to go to sleep now. I'm at the hospital at 5 a.m.

Max rolls over on to his side.

MIMI

What are we going to do tomorrow?

MAX

Go to the hospital. What do you mean?

MIMI

Apart from that. I'm a tourist. I want you to show me around. I need to do some shopping as well. I mean, I've only got twenty-four hours.

CUT TO:

EXT. NEW YORK STREETS. PRE-DAWN

Max walking to the hospital.

CUT TO:

INT. CHARLIE'S HOSPITAL ROOM. DAWN

Charlie's breathing is laboured and painful. Max watches as the nurses do their thing.

He is amazed at the endurance of this human body. Charlie and Max look at each other. Despite the pain Charlie raises his eyebrows and smiles.

DISSOLVE TO:

INT. CHARLIE'S HOSPITAL ROOM. DAY

Charlie is asleep. Max is alone in the room with him. We hear footsteps in the corridor. A well-dressed Man of about sixty comes to the doorway of the room. He doesn't come close to the bed but stares at the sleeping Charlie. He and Max look at each other. The Man turns and walks out of the room, his footsteps slower, receding, and then the room is silent again.

DISSOLVE TO:

INT. CHARLIE'S HOSPITAL ROOM. NIGHT

Once again the room is full. The same crowd. Faces we recognize. As cheerful as ever but the strain is evident on everyone. Charlie, in new blue silk pyjamas, is propped up and listening to some gossip. On his knees is a theatre plan with a lighting rig marked out. Charlie is making adjustments on his design for a show that is moving from one space to another. His assistant, Kevin, is taking notes.

Max looks around the room. No sign of Vernon or Karen. Mimi thumbs through a Vanity Fair *magazine. She is surrounded by shopping bags from department stores.*

DISSOLVE TO:

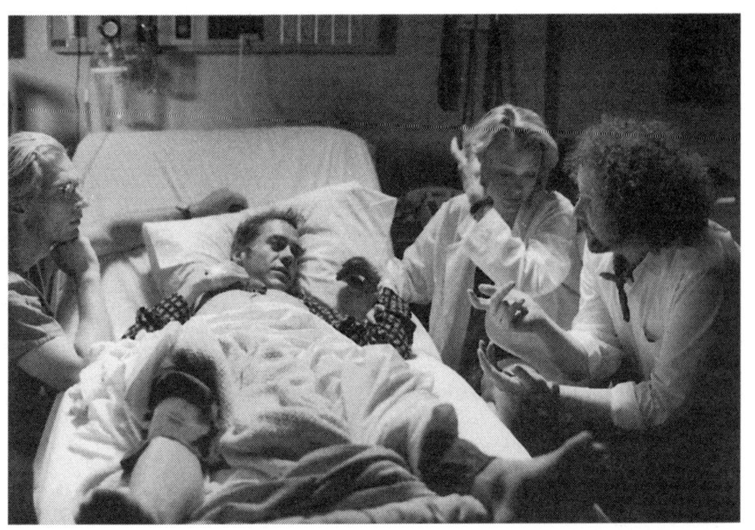

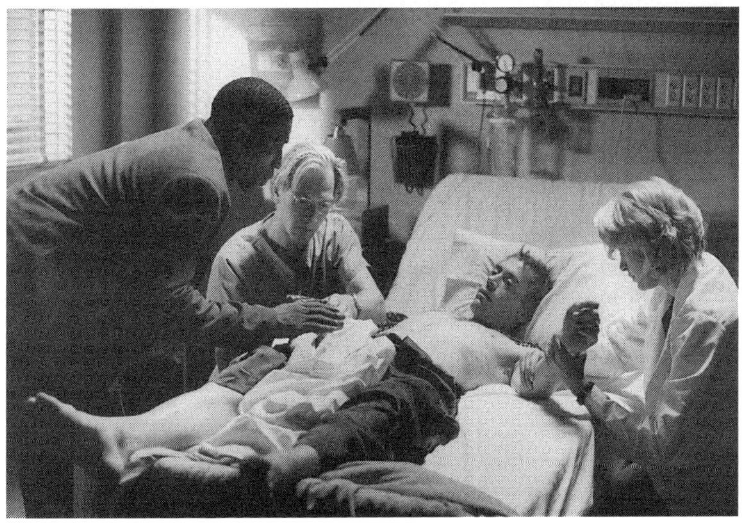

EXT. HOTEL. NIGHT

Mimi gets into a taxi. Max kisses her and helps her with her bags.

MIMI

Well . . . I guess I'll see you at the . . .

MAX

Funeral? It's not necessary.

MIMI

Don't make me sound so bad. I'll be there.

MAX

Kiss the kids for me, OK.

CUT TO:

INT. HOSPITAL CORRIDORS. PRE-DAWN

Max arrives at Charlie's door and says hello to the Nurse on duty. He gives her a box of chocolates. Most of the lights are off and the room is lit only by one night-light from the corridor. Max opens the door carefully and creeps in.

INT. CHARLIE'S HOSPITAL ROOM. PRE-DAWN

Charlie is sleeping fitfully with his mask on. A compressor hisses gently and some classical music from an all-night station can be heard faintly. Max sits down in a chair and leans back to rest his tired bones. He rubs his eyes and stretches his neck.

KAREN

(*really quietly*)

Hi.

Max freezes and then looks around the darkened room. There is a figure in another chair on the other side of the bed. The following dialogue is almost whispered.

MAX

When did you get back?

KAREN

Last night. Vernon had to leave this morning so we called in last night to see how he was . . . which was not so good . . . so I stayed with him.

MAX

All night?

KAREN

Yes. I'm going to go now.

But she doesn't make a move yet. Max's eyes get used to the dark and now he can make out her features. (I'd like to approximate this feeling with the camera exposure . . . slowly open up the iris.)

MAX

You must be exhausted.

KAREN

Yeah, but it's OK.

(*long pause*)

I liked your wife. She's very beautiful.

MAX

She liked you too.

Karen smiles at Max. She doesn't buy this for a moment. She looks at Charlie.

How was he?

KAREN

We had a good night. He talked a lot.

MAX

What about?

KAREN

Everything. We talked about you. He really loves you.

MAX

He digs you too. He told me.

They both look at Charlie. Silence for a while.

KAREN

He told me that you went to see him last year and I realized that it was that same time . . .

MAX

Yes. The day I saw you in the hotel.

(*longish pause*)

Is this very awkward for you?

KAREN

No, it's OK. We're both adults. You have a beautiful wife . . .

MAX

And you have a terrific husband. I mean it. Vernon is a great guy.

KAREN

Thank you, he is a great guy. So . . . we just have to be mature about this. As far as I'm concerned . . .

(*looks away*)

. . . nothing happened.

MAX

Exactly. That's right. Nothing happened.

Max stares at her until she meets his gaze.

KAREN

Well . . . I guess I should go and get some sleep.

She gets up and Max gets up also. To get to the door she has to pass him. They're both wondering whether to shake hands or what.

MAX

See you later.

Max leans in and kisses her on the cheek, his hands on her shoulders. They hold this for a beat and then something happens and he kisses her on the mouth for a long time. At first she doesn't respond and then she does and her arms go around his neck. They part and she touches his face with her hand.

There is a change in the sound of the respirator. They look at the bed.

Angle – Charlie is awake and staring at them. He takes the mask off and smiles weakly.

CHARLIE

Max . . . Karen, good morning.

Max and Karen look at each other.

KAREN

Good morning, Charlie. New shift is here.

And she goes to kiss Charlie goodbye.

Bye. See you tonight.

And she leaves. Max goes to the door and watches her walk out of his sight down the corridor, then he brings his chair close to the bed. Nothing is said for a while. Charlie again takes off his mask but keeps it in his hand in case he has to use it. He looks at Max.

CHARLIE

So?

MAX

What?

CHARLIE

Don't fuck with me, Max. I'm too tired. What . . . are . . . you doing kissing my sister-in-law? And why was she asking about you last night? Spit it out.

Max takes a deep breath.

MAX

OK . . . last year, when I was here for that convention . . .

etc., etc.

Music comes in and washes over Max's tale.

Camera moves into a close-up on Charlie.

(*voice-over*)

. . . so I told him everything.

INT. CHARLIE'S HOSPITAL ROOM. DAY

Time cut back on to Max.

MAX

So . . . what should I do?

CHARLIE

Life is an orange, Max.

MAX

What's that mean?

CHARLIE

You don't remember that joke? The young Jewish boy sitting at the feet of his wise father, who says to him, 'Always remember, son, life is an orange.' And all his life he thinks and ponders on the meaning of this phrase. Sixty years later his father is dying and he goes to visit him for the last time and as his father is slipping away he says to him, 'What does it mean, Pa?' and his dad says, 'What does what mean, son?' And he says . . . you know . . . 'Life is an orange' . . . and with his last breath he says . . . 'I have no idea.'

MAX

Right.

CHARLIE

Vernon is not coming back for a couple of days. Is Mimi still here?

MAX

No.

CHARLIE

Then you have a short time to work this thing out. But you have to spend some time together. You gotta work your shit out, Max.

Max takes Charlie's hand.

That bad stuff between you and me, Max, that was a stupid waste of time . . .

MAX

No, I was . . .

CHARLIE

You were right. I was envious. Envy is a horrible thing, you know. I was hurt because you didn't take me with you.

MAX

I tried to, Charlie. I didn't know how. I didn't have the power . . .

CHARLIE

I understand. I just wanted to say it. I just wanted us to be clean again.

Max is overcome with emotion. He tries to hold it in but it's a losing battle and he begins to cry. Charlie strokes his hand.

MAX

I'm sorry.

CHARLIE

Don't be. This thing is much harder for my friends than it is for me.

MAX

Listen, I have to ask you something. Do you want to talk to a priest?

CHARLIE

(*firm*)

No way. I've seen too many of my friends lose their courage at the last moment. I mean, I'm frightened, I am frightened, but I'm also fascinated by what happens next. So, thanks, but no thanks.

MAX

I had to ask.

CHARLIE

I know.

After a longish pause . . .

MAX

Your dad was here.

They sit in silence for the longest time and then Charlie puts his mask back on. He looks at Max and Max looks at him. He takes Max's hand and squeezes it.

CUT TO:

BLACK SCREEN.

In the black we hear sombre church music played on an organ.

MAX
(*voice-over*)
There's something about funerals that is not in the slightest bit depressing. Which is not to say that they're not sad. But what they really are is deeply erotic . . .

FADE UP FROM BLACK . . .

EXT. HIGHWAY WITH VIEW TO MANHATTAN. DAY

Charlie's funeral procession departs from the city.

INT. NEW ENGLAND CHURCH. DAY

Camera moves around and finds faces and images. Everyone looks great. Every gay man, every actor, Max, Mimi, Vernon, Karen, Charlie's sisters, the Nuns and the Priest. The sunlight is streaming through the windows of the church and the incense smoke is hanging in the air, giving the location a legitimate Ridley Scott feel. One of the actors, a beautiful black man with a voice like Ray Charles, is singing one of Charlie's favourite songs. Something like 'Drown in My Own Tears'. The organ gives a light backing which is augmented by an alto sax and a guitar. Most importantly the music is sexy. A photograph of Charlie laughing has been blown up and is the centrepiece of the altar.

Everyone is dressed in black and white. Costume and make-up are of crucial importance here. The women have gone to town: black dresses, black stockings (with seams), veils, pale make-up (but a touch of red to the lips).

MAX
(*voice-over*)
. . . there was a combination of factors at work on that Wednesday. Charlie's friends were mainly actors or theatrical types, and they see every situation as a script or a play. Given the nature of a funeral and all the black and white that is required . . . that would be like . . . a Bergman film . . . or maybe a Visconti. Plus something else which is out of all our control . . . funerals are sexy. Everyone dressed up to the

nines . . . tears trickling down cheeks, everyone kneeling and taking part in a pagan ritual. And most importantly, the brain, having been informed that one of the population just died, is screaming at the male and female reproductive organs . . . go and make babies, keep the human race going. In the case of Charlie's friends that meant some confused and mixed signals were flying around the venue.

Montage of shots as the ceremony progresses. Grief and sex. Women crying, men taking them by the arm and leading them down the aisle, everyone looking sexy.

Karen and Vernon are sitting in front of Max and Mimi, and as they kneel for a prayer, Max stares at her profile and the back of her neck, the back of her knees, the seam of her stockings.

Mimi has not been fashion-shy either and her tight black dress, cut very short, shows off her black-stockinged legs to great effect. Her hair is up in a severe style but the short veil frames her long neck beautifully. Vernon turns and smiles and nods hello. Max is about to respond when he realizes that Vernon is in fact looking at Mimi. Max turns to Mimi but she closes her eyes and bows her head in prayer.

CUT TO:

INT. NEW ENGLAND CHURCH (LATER). DAY

Vernon saying a few words to the congregation.

VERNON

. . . and we'll always remember him as that little kid on the beach, a kid who had dreams of hitting the big time on Broadway. I remember one day, coming home from school and seeing Charlie coming out of our mother's room, dressed in one of her outfits . . .

At this point some of the people decide Vernon is funny, others decide he is tasteless, others wish he would move it on because he has already been talking for ten minutes.

. . . anyway . . . it was Charlie's last wish that we have a celebration at our house. It's all paid for by Charlie, it's what he wanted . . .

(*chokes up*)

. . . so, see you there.

Angle – Mimi. Very moved by the speech, tears in her eyes.

CUT TO:

EXT. THE GROUNDS OF A BEAUTIFUL HOUSE NEAR THE CHURCH. DAY

The shot opens on a close-up of a For Sale notice pinned to a tree next to the entrance to the drive.

A car drives past and pulls up next to the big house. The garden is overgrown and uncared for. Max, Vernon, Karen and Mimi get out of the car. Three of them go into the house. Max does not. Other cars begin arriving and parking. Max walks off around the side of the house.

CUT TO:

EXT. REAR OF THE HOUSE. DAY

Max walks up to the camera and looks beyond at something.

Angle – Max's POV. A dilapidated child's house, not a bought house but something that has been made specially. It is a simple copy of the main house. The glass in one of the windows has been broken. Max walks up to the house and tries the door. It opens. He goes in.

CUT TO:

INT. CHILD'S HOUSE. DAY

It is gloomy inside but we can make out small furniture and a camp bed against a wall. Posters and things on the wall. Maybe a photograph or two. Something that ties in Max and Charlie and maybe even Vernon. Camera moves in tight on Max's face.

CUT TO:

EXT. MAIN HOUSE. NIGHT

A locked-off camera transition shot from dusk to night of the party beginning.

INT. MAIN HOUSE. NIGHT

The wake is in progress. The drink is flowing and a loud band is playing, making conversation difficult. Everyone is taking Charlie's last wish seriously and trying to have a good time.

This sequence is as much to do with camera and sound, Max watching people and in particular Karen. Joints are being passed around. Serious bonding is taking place on the dance floor.

Karen dances with Vernon, watched by Max. We can see by Max's face that he is jealous.

Vernon says something to Karen and she laughs. Max pours himself a large Scotch and is joined by Mimi.

Vernon and Karen come off the dance floor and she goes out of the room and into the kitchen, while Vernon joins Max and Mimi. The music seems louder than ever. Vernon asks Mimi to dance and Max is left alone, sulking. He walks out of the room.

INT. KITCHEN. NIGHT

Karen is washing some glasses at the sink as Max comes in. At first she doesn't hear him and then she senses that someone is watching her and turns around. They look at each other and someone else comes in for a Coke from the fridge. They pay no heed to him and he leaves. Max walks over to the sink and touches her face. She kisses his hand and then they are kissing for the longest time. Her hands are around his neck tight and then they go limp and she slides down him in a dead faint.

Angle – Max kneels next to her as she comes to. She looks at him, almost as if she hated him, and gets up and walks a little unsteadily to the sink.

CUT TO:

INT. MAIN ROOM. NIGHT

As Max comes into the room Vernon and Mimi are just coming off the floor. They walk to Max and start talking and then are joined by some other people. Mimi says something to Max which he doesn't hear. She leans in closer.

MIMI

I'm going to lie down for a while. I don't feel very well.

MAX

Do you want me to come with you?

MIMI

No, it's OK. I won't be long.

And she exits. Across the other side of the room Karen is talking to some women. Max cannot take his eyes off her but she refuses to look at him. Someone hands Max a joint and he takes it. He offers it to Vernon and to his surprise Vernon accepts and takes a deep drag before excusing himself.

VERNON

I'd better check on the kitchen.

And Vernon exits. More people join Max's group, the music gets even louder and Max feels more alone than ever in his life. He stares at Karen but she will not even turn her head in his direction. A man asks her to dance and leads her to the floor. Max finds it almost unbearable to see her with another man, despite the fact that the man is one of Charlie's gay friends. He loses the struggle for control of his emotions and walks on to the floor and cuts in on Karen and her partner. The man exits good-humouredly but Karen seems angry with Max and walks away. Max follows and takes her by the arm firmly. She tries to break free but his grip is tight. Without breaking his stride, Max hustles her out of the room and towards the front door, which is open.

CUT TO:

EXT. HOUSE. NIGHT

Max drags Karen out of the house. She is not completely resisting. She's trying to look pissed but a smile breaks out on her face.

KAREN

What do you think you're doing? You are a lunatic.

Max is not smiling. He seems angry. He's still hustling her away from the front of the house. They go around the side and stop, she leaning against the wooden side of the house. He lets go of her and walks away before turning around and looking at her. She meets his gaze this time.

What do you want of me, Max?

MAX

I want to see your legs.

Karen thinks about this for a while. We can hear the music from the band mixing with the crickets in the garden. A night bird sings, maybe a nightingale. It's a full moon but there is light cloud and . . .

Angle – the sky. A cloud goes over the moon.

Angle – Max's POV of Karen. We can just make her out in the dark. She slowly lifts her skirt up.

Higher.

The skirt goes higher.

CUT TO:

EXT. CHILD'S HOUSE. NIGHT

Two silhouettes approach the house. By the door they merge and kiss passionately. Clothes are being opened, zippers unzipped.

CUT TO:

INT. CHILD'S HOUSE. NIGHT

The door opens and the two figures are framed in the doorway for a moment. They are almost making love. Their impatience to be making love is clear. The door is kicked shut and in the dark we can tell that they are against the wall. She is moaning and he is pulling her clothes off. Then there is a sigh of pure ecstasy from both of them.

KAREN

Oh, Max, I've missed you so much.

CUT TO:

EXT. SKY. NIGHT

The cloud starts to reveal the big bright moon.

CUT TO:

INT. CHILD'S HOUSE. NIGHT

Slowly the room is filled with a beautiful silver light. Max and Karen are making love against the wall.

Strange high wide-angle of the room. It takes us a while to make this angle out. Also the room is still dark but getting brighter all the time as the moon is revealed. We become aware of the fact that not only are Max and Karen making love against the wall but . . . there is another couple on the bed. The man is lying between the woman's legs and his pants are around his ankles.

CUT TO:

Tight angle on Karen. She is framed by Max's shoulder against the wall. Her eyes are closed and she is kissing his neck. Her eyes open and she sees . . .

The couple on the bed.

Close-up – it is Mimi and she is staring at Karen. The man turns his head and we see that it is Vernon.

Reverse angle. Max becomes aware and turns to see.

Cut between the angles. Everyone looking at everyone else.

FADE TO BLACK.

SUBTITLES IN BLACK: EXACTLY ONE YEAR LATER

FADE UP FROM BLACK:

INT. NEW YORK RESTAURANT. DAY

Quite an old-fashioned place. A string quartet play a selection of waltzes. We see Max come in. It seems that he's late, because he is hurrying. Camera moves backwards with him as he sees his table and waves.

MAX

Hi . . . sorry I'm late.

He sits down and we see that he's meeting Vernon, Karen and Mimi. Mimi looks pissed that he's late. They are all looking at the menu. Max picks one up and scans it.

CUT TO:

INT. NEW YORK RESTAURANT (LATER). DAY

They are all eating and talking. Everything seems cool. Friendly, but not too friendly. It is very difficult to get a handle on what the situation is. It's as if nothing ever happened.

However, if you were to analyse this scene you would notice that Max talks to Vernon or Karen talks to Mimi, but the men and the women do not talk to each other.

Max watches the two women talking to each other.

CUT TO:

INT. NEW YORK RESTAURANT (LATER). DAY

Drinking coffee. Mimi looks at her watch. Max signals the waiter and does a 'Bring me the check' mime.

VERNON

Are we in a hurry?

MAX

Gotta pick up the kids from the cinema.

MIMI

A film I thought was completely unsuitable.

CUT TO:

Two credit cards are tossed on to the plate with the bill.

CUT TO:

EXT. RESTAURANT. TAXI STAND. DAY

The four of them stand waiting for a taxi. One pulls up.

VERNON

Maybe we should share a cab. What direction are you going in?

MAX

It's way out of your way. You take this one.

VERNON

I thought you were in a hurry.

MAX

We have time. It's nice to be in the fresh air for a while.

VERNON

(*laughing*)

If you can call this fresh air.

MAX

Fresher than LA at least.

VERNON

You're right there. Good to see you, Max.

MAX

You too, Vern.

The two women kiss and then . . .

Max kisses Mimi while Karen kisses Vernon.

Vernon and Mimi get into the taxi together. Max closes the door but Mimi opens the window.

MIMI

Make sure the kids are properly packed this time.

MAX

Don't worry.

MIMI

Last time they left half their stuff with you. And you'll bring them straight to the airport? The flight is at one.

Karen looks pissed at Mimi for making the scene but keeps silent.

MAX

They'll be there. See you tomorrow.

The cab drives off.

KAREN

She had to make her point.

Karen and Max look at each other. They both seem older, tired. Max puts his arm around her, gives her a hug and kisses the top of her head.

We hear the slow movement from the Beethoven quartet.

Camera moves in tight on the two heads. Max becomes fascinated by the delicate hair on the back of Karen's neck and kisses her there.

FADE TO BLACK.

PORTRAITS

I thought it would be interesting to do a formal portrait of everyone who worked on the film. Here are a few examples.

Wesley Snipes

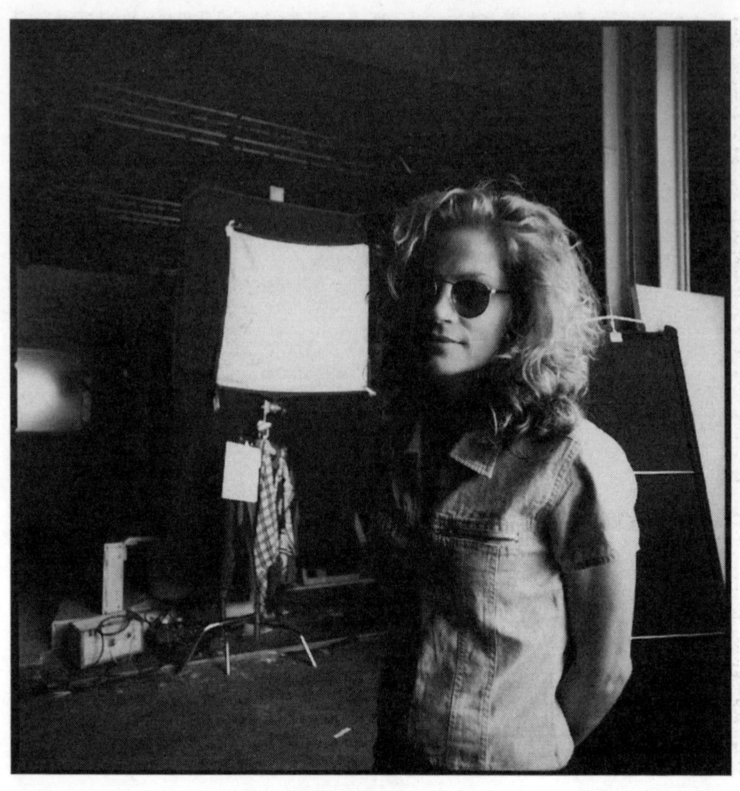

Annie Stewart (Producer)

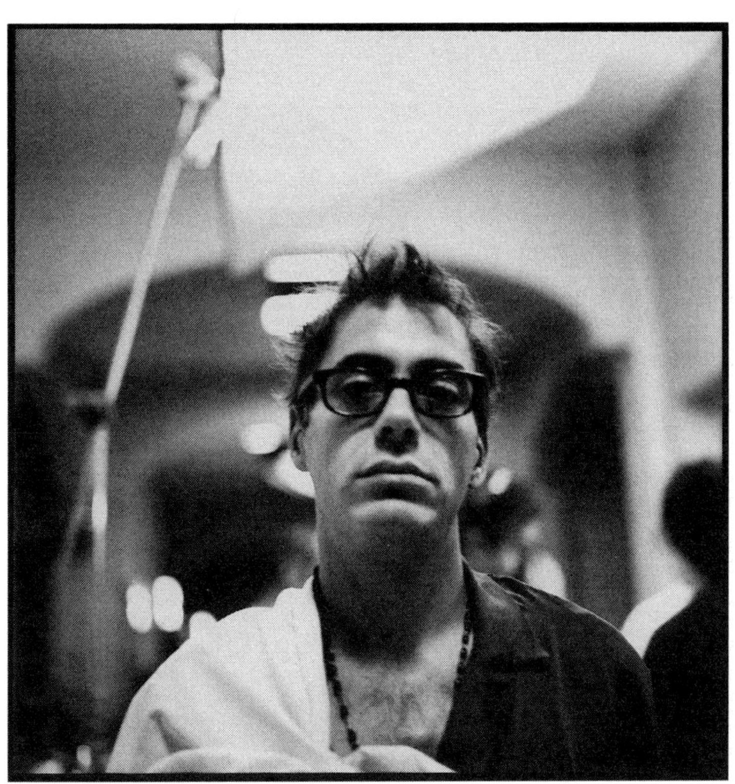

Robert Downey Jr

Kyle Maclachlan

Thomas Hayden Church

Xander Berkely

Julian Sands

John Ratzenberger

Vincent Ward